ÆBLESKIVER

A NEW TAKE ON TRADITIONAL DANISH PANCAKES

ÆBLESKIVER

A NEW TAKE ON TRADITIONAL DANISH PANCAKES

PIM PAULINE OVERGAARD

THE
collective
BOOK STUDIO

Library of Congress Cataloging-in-Publication Data available.
ISBN: 978-1-68555-792-8
Ebook ISBN: 978-1-68555-059-2
Library of Congress Control Number: 2024901884

Printed using Forest Stewardship Council certified stock from
sustainably managed forests.

Manufactured in China.

10 9 8 7 6 5 4 3 2 1

The Collective Book Studio®
Oakland, California
www.thecollectivebook.studio

CONTENTS

INTRODUCTION

FULL DISCLOSURE—I'M NOT DANISH . . .

In fact, I'm half Swedish, half Norwegian, and I was born and raised in Sweden. In addition, I have spent the last thirty years in California. In my defense, I did go to school in Copenhagen, and I absolutely love Denmark. Copenhagen is still my favorite city in Scandinavia, and I go back often.

Surprisingly, few Swedes know that æbleskiver even exist. Interestingly, it was not until I moved to San Francisco that I first heard about them, and even more so when I visited the Danish town of Solvang in Southern California. Seems like Americans know more about æbleskiver than Swedes do.

Æbleskiver are fascinating in their simplicity and potential. A plate of æbleskiver can be as basic as simple pancakes served with butter and syrup or with jam and whipped cream. They can also be closer in texture and flavor to muffins or rolls—the possibilities are endless. Sweet or savory, they can be served any time of day, from breakfast to brunch, lunch, dinner, and dessert.

About fifteen years ago, two of my cousins were diagnosed with celiac disease. Back then, it wasn't as easy to find gluten-free products as it is now. That's when I created the Scandelicious brand, focusing on Scandinavian, gluten-free breakfast mixes, such as Swedish pancakes, Swedish waffles (the sweetheart kind), and Danish æbleskiver. Since then, the recognition of various dietary needs has increased significantly. Offering guests dietary alternatives, while considering social preference, taste, and allergies, is immensely satisfying. To me, creating happiness with delicious food and healing bodies with nutritious food is love, and that's why this book includes æbleskiver recipes that are gluten-free, vegan, and much more.

. . . AND I'M NOT A CHEF.

Although my interest—some call it obsession—with food has been obvious since birth, professionally I chose a path within fashion and interior design with a focus on textiles, print, and pattern. My passion is in creativity, with a strong dose of perseverance and a wish to inspire. As head designer at Williams Sonoma Home, occasionally working across brands with GreenRow, Pottery Barn, and Williams Sonoma (kitchen), I'm spoiled with opportunities to conceptualize and create for a variety of exciting projects. Although I often lean toward the edgy and unique, I find the most gratifying designs to be a balance of traditional and contemporary, classic and offbeat. It has become quite clear that I naturally approach cooking and recipe making in a similar way.

My great interest and curiosity around food has stayed consistent throughout my whole life. From watching my grandmother prepare traditional Scandinavian dishes from scratch, to having a dad who continuously and without hesitation let me make up my own recipes (even when it became obvious nothing edible would ever come of it), to starting a recipe blog and creating the Scandelicious food brand, I have always loved food and cooking.

All these experiences combined—my love of food, Scandinavian heritage, excitement for things that are edgy and inspiring, and desire for inclusion—have brought me here, to an expression of taste and style, rooted in Scandinavian tradition, with recipes for everyone.

SPECIAL DIETS

The recipes are all marked to indicate if they are:

NF = Nut-free	VG = Vegetarian
GF = Gluten-free	V = Vegan

ONE ÆBLESKIVE, TWO ÆBLESKIVER

Historically, slices of apple were dipped in pancake batter and fried, explaining the origin of the name *æbleskiver* (pronounced EE-bleh-skewr), which literally means "apple slices." (*Æble* = apple, and *skiver* = slices.) The word *æbleskive* is singular and *æbleskiver* is plural. Although it's tempting to add an "s" at the end, "æbleskivers" is grammatically incorrect. Over time, the name stayed the same, but the recipe evolved, and now æbleskiver can include other ingredients, not just apples. But, they will always be in the shape of a more or less symmetrical sphere. Because of my Scandinavian roots, many of the flavor combinations in this book originate from my own food memories and the region's culinary traditions.

PANS AND TOOLS

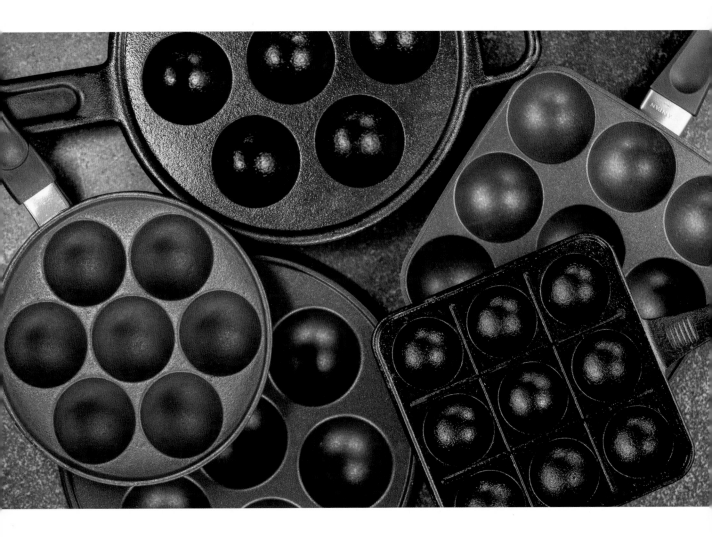

Old stories tell of Vikings returning from battle and using their banged-up shields over an open fire as the first æbleskiver pans. Even the pans first created specifically to make æbleskiver are said to be made from copper and are more than three hundred years old. Copper was later replaced by cast iron, often the preferred material used today. Some electric models are available as well, but few have multiple settings, making it tricky to get evenly cooked æbleskiver, so I don't recommend them. Nonstick models can be a plus for egg-less batters, which tend to stick more to the pan than those with eggs, and for special diets that avoid butter or oil.

The Danes are not the only ones using a hemispherical pan to make globe-shaped pancakes. While writing this book, I found myself inspired by many different cultures, some more obvious than others. Japan is known for their takoyaki octopus balls, often found as street food there and all over Asia. Holland is known for their sweet poffertjes, and India for their sweet gulab jamun and savory paniyaram, to name a few.

As a result of the countless varieties of pancakes found all around the world, the selection of pans can seem endless. The pan sizes and cavity sizes vary, as do the number of cavities in each pan. From 1- to 2 ½-inch wells, with 5 to 25 wells per pan, the home versions are priced from $15 to $150. To create the characteristic globe-shaped pancakes, the pans must have the complete half sphere shaped wells. The most common Danish æbleskiver pan is round with one handle and has seven cavities, each 2 to 2¼ inches (5 to 5.5 cm) wide, and that is the one I used to create the recipes in this book. The yields of the recipes reflect this (they are in multiples of seven) and may be different for you if your pan size is different. If you don't happen to have an æbleskiver pan, that's okay. Most of the recipes in this book can be cooked in a regular frying pan like American pancakes. They won't have the fun round shape, but they will still taste delicious.

Ice cream scoops are ideal to use for scooping up the batter. Use one that is about the same width as the cavities in your pan to fill them up, and also have a smaller one to top off the æbleskiver with batter before turning them to close them up. For the typical Danish pans, one 2¼-inch (5.5-cm) scoop and one ¾- to 1-inch (2- to 2.5-cm) scoop are perfect. For pans with smaller, 1½- to 1¾-inch (4- to 4.5-cm) cavities, a 1½-inch (4-cm) scoop is an excellent addition.

Traditionally, a knitting needle was used to turn the æbleskiver in the pan, and many people still prefer that to anything else. You can buy specially shaped wooden turning tools made for this purpose, and they are often sold in pairs. I suggest using 6- to 8-inch (15- to 20-cm) bamboo sticks or skewers, which will do the job, are inexpensive, and often come in packages of several hundred.

HOW TO MAKE THE PERFECT SPHERE

Don't be intimidated by the impressive-looking sphere shapes of the æbleskiver. When you use a traditional æbleskiver pan, they are actually very easy to make. To get perfect spheres, the cavities in the pan should be half-sphere shaped. Some pans have cavities with a flat bottom, and if you have one of those, they won't make the same shape you'll see here, but they will be just as tasty. If that's the case, you simply turn the æebleskiver over a few times to complete cooking.

Low to medium heat is a good range for most recipes, mostly depending on the difference in pan sensitivity and stove accuracy, but also on how some ingredients need more time to cook. The first time you try a new recipe, start on the lower end to make sure you don't end up with burnt æbleskiver with an uncooked center.

Recipes using yeast or sourdough do well cooked a bit slower, on lower heat. Since they need a little more space to expand, you want to avoid closing them up too quickly, in turn making them unnecessarily dense.

1. Place the pan over low to medium heat and add ½ teaspoon of butter or oil to each cavity. Let the butter melt until it starts to bubble.

2. Pour enough batter into each cavity to fill it almost to the top. The batter will expand and create a small "muffin top." Ice cream scoops are great tools for pouring in the batter (see Pans and Tools, page 8). If you're making filled æbleskiver, fill the cavities a little less, no more than halfway, before adding the filling. Lightly cover the filling with more batter to get the same result.

3. Use a wooden skewer to turn the æbleskiver 90°. You will know when they are ready to turn by poking them all the way through, and gently turn the skewer. They will turn easily when they are ready, and the uncooked batter will pour to the bottom.

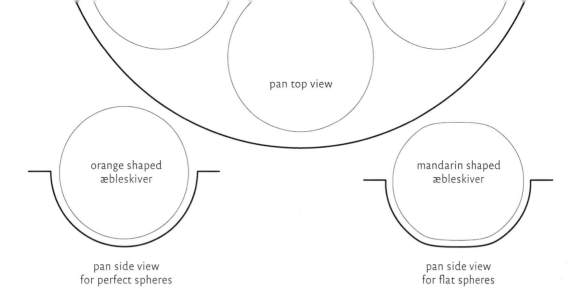

pan top view

orange shaped
æbleskiver

mandarin shaped
æbleskiver

pan side view
for perfect spheres

pan side view
for flat spheres

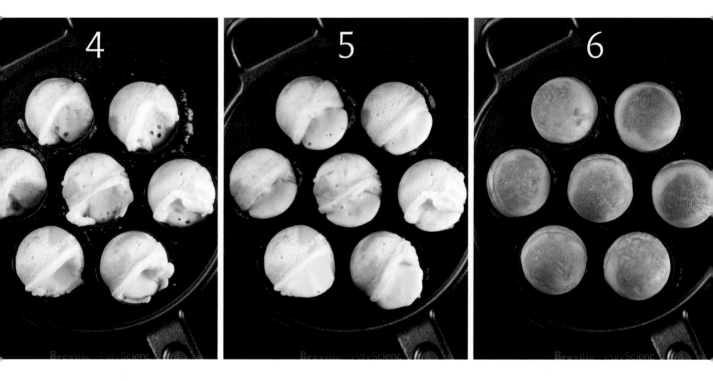

4. Turn the æbleskiver another 90° in a different direction to continue to close up the sphere. Lift up the æbleskiver while turning and tuck in the overflow.

5. Unless the uncooked batter already fills the cavities to the top, add a little bit more batter to top them off before turning to close them up. Lift and turn to move the opening to the bottom of the pan.

6. Turn the æbleskiver to close them up and continue to turn until golden all around. They are cooked all the way through when a small wooden skewer or toothpick inserted in the center comes out mostly clean. Serve right away or keep the æbleskiver warm in a 200°F (100°C) oven.

BASIC
RECIPES

FLAVORING CHART

Use the Basic Recipes as a starting point for your own creations. Whether you want to flavor the batter or add a filling, you can use the following flavoring chart as a guide and for inspiration.

FLAVORINGS	IN BATTER Per one batch	FILLING Per one pancake
CHOCOLATE	½ to 1 cup (85 to 170 g) chips or chunks; gently fold in at the end	1 to 1½ teaspoons paste like Nutella or ganache
JAM OR CURD	½ cup (120 g); gently fold in at the end	1 to 1½ teaspoons
BERRIES	½ to 1 cup (75 to 150 g); gently fold in at the end	1 to 2 berries
FRUIT	½ to 1 cup (75 to 150 g) cubed; gently fold in at the end	½-inch (1.3-cm) cubes
NUTS	½ to 1 cup (75 to 150 g) chopped; gently fold in at the end	1 to 2 nuts or 1 to 1½ teaspoons nut butter
ESSENCES AND EXTRACTS	1 to 2 teaspoons; add to wet ingredients	n/a
FRESH HERBS	3 tablespoons finely chopped; add with wet ingredients	Mix ¾ cup (180 g) cream cheese with ¼ cup (10 to 15 g) finely chopped herbs and add 1 to 1½ teaspoons per pancake
CHEESE AND TOFU	1 cup (120 g) cubed or grated; gently fold in at the end	½ inch (12 mm) cubes
VEGETABLES	½ to 1 cup (60 to 120 g) grated, raw, or cooked; gently fold in at the end	1½ teaspoons cubed or grated, raw or cooked
BACON, HAM, OR SAUSAGE	½ to 1 cup (75 to 150 g) chopped, cooked or cured; gently fold in at the end	1½ teaspoons finely chopped, cooked, or cured
COCOA POWDER	3 tablespoons; add to dry ingredients	Mix to taste with ¾ cup (180 g) marzipan, nut butter, or cream cheese and add 1 to 1½ teaspoons per pancake
GROUND CINNAMON	1 tablespoon; add to dry ingredients	Mix ¾ cup (180 g) marzipan, nut butter, ganache, or cream cheese with 1 tablespoon ground cinnamon and add 1 to 1½ teaspoons per pancake
FRESH CITRUS	Zest and juice from ½ fruit; add to wet ingredients	1 to 1½ teaspoons citrus-flavored curd or custard
VANILLA	Seeds from 1 vanilla bean or ½ teaspoon extract added to wet ingredients, or 1 teaspoon vanilla sugar added to dry ingredients	1½ teaspoons vanilla custard

CLASSIC ÆBLESKIVER

This is one of the easiest recipes to follow and the most foolproof. If you are in doubt about where to begin, and there are no particular dietary needs you must adhere to, this is a good starting place. It is also the most forgiving to use when experimenting with flavorings, whether the flavors are mixed in the batter or used as a filling. The sugar is optional but will add only a little bit of sweetness. Even for savory combinations, a dash of sugar will enhance and balance the flavors.

Makes 21 æbleskiver | NF | VG

2¼ cups (315 g) all-purpose flour

1 tablespoon baking powder

½ teaspoon salt

2 tablespoons sugar (optional)

2 cups (480 ml) milk or buttermilk

2 large eggs

**2 tablespoons melted butter +
more for the pan**

Combine the flour, baking powder, salt, and sugar (if using) in a medium bowl and mix well. Set aside.

In a separate bowl, lightly mix together the milk, eggs, and 2 tablespoons of melted butter with a fork. Pour the mixture over the dry ingredients and stir quickly until just combined. Try not to stir the batter again after this.

Heat the æbleskiver pan over low to medium heat with about ½ teaspoon of butter in each cavity. Using an ice cream scoop or a spoon, fill each cavity almost to the top.

Cook until a crust forms on the batter. Using a thin wooden skewer, turn the æbleskiver 90°, letting the batter spill over. Once a skin has formed, the æbleskiver will turn easily. Turn again in a different direction and then a last time to close up the sphere. Spin the æbleskiver around until evenly golden brown and cooked all the way through. Serve right away or keep the æbleskiver warm in a 200°F (100°C) oven.

GLUTEN-FREE ÆBLESKIVER

Whether you're living gluten-free, are curious to try, or are cooking for a guest, this is an easy recipe that results in æbleskiver very close to the classic. In the event you're cooking for a guest, ask whether your guest is sensitive to cross-contamination. The sugar is optional but will add only a little bit of sweetness. Even for savory combinations, a dash of sugar will enhance and balance the flavors.

Makes 21 æbleskiver | NF | GF

1¼ cups (175 g) sweet rice flour
½ cup (70 g) brown rice flour
½ cup (90 g) potato starch
¼ cup (30 g) tapioca starch
2 tablespoons buttermilk powder
2 tablespoons psyllium husk
1 teaspoon guar gum
1 tablespoon baking powder
½ teaspoon salt
2 tablespoons sugar (optional)
2 cups (480 ml) milk or buttermilk
2 large eggs
2 tablespoons melted butter + more for the pan

Combine the sweet rice flour, brown rice flour, potato starch, tapioca starch, buttermilk powder, psyllium husk, guar gum, baking powder, salt, and sugar (if using) in a medium bowl and mix well. Set aside.

In a separate bowl, lightly mix together the milk, eggs, and 2 tablespoons of melted butter with a fork. Pour the mixture over the dry ingredients and whisk quickly, until just combined. Try not to stir the batter again after this.

Heat the æbleskiver pan over low to medium heat with about ½ teaspoon of butter in each cavity. Using an ice cream scoop or a spoon, fill each cavity almost to the top.

Cook until a crust forms on the batter. Using a thin wooden skewer, turn the æbleskiver 90°, letting the batter spill over. Once a skin has formed, the æbleskiver will turn easily. Turn again in a different direction and then a last time to close up the sphere. Spin the æbleskiver around until evenly golden brown and cooked all the way through. Serve right away or keep the æbleskiver warm in a 200°F (100°C) oven.

VEGAN ÆBLESKIVER

Having tried many egg alternatives for this recipe, I found applesauce, sweetened or unsweetened, to work especially well. The sweetened version is more neutral in flavor, while the unsweetened adds a little bit of tartness, but either one works well. If you have a different favorite substitute, feel free to exchange the applesauce for the equivalent of two eggs. Similarly, using a plant-based butter results in æbleskiver closest to the classic, but any plant-based cooking oil can be used in its place. The sugar is optional but will add only a little bit of sweetness. Even for savory combinations, a dash of sugar will enhance and balance the flavors.

Makes 21 æbleskiver | V

2¼ cups (315 g) all-purpose flour

2 tablespoons psyllium husk

1 tablespoon baking powder

½ teaspoon salt

2 tablespoons sugar (optional)

2 cups (480 ml) plant milk

½ cup (120 g) unsweetened applesauce

2 tablespoons melted plant-based butter + more for the pan

Combine the flour, psyllium husk, baking powder, salt, and sugar (if using) in a medium bowl and mix well. Set aside.

In a separate bowl, lightly mix together the plant milk, applesauce, and 2 tablespoons of plant-based butter with a fork. Pour the mixture over the dry ingredients and whisk quickly, until just combined. Try not to stir the batter again after this.

Heat the æbleskiver pan over low to medium heat with about ½ teaspoon of melted plant-based butter in each cavity. Using an ice cream scoop or a spoon, fill each cavity almost to the top.

Cook until a crust forms on the batter. Using a thin wooden skewer, turn the æbleskiver 90°, letting the batter spill over. Once a skin has formed, the æbleskiver will turn easily. Turn again in a different direction and then a last time to close up the sphere. Spin the æbleskiver around until evenly golden brown and cooked all the way through. Serve right away or keep the æbleskiver warm in a 200°F (100°C) oven.

VEGAN AND GLUTEN-FREE ÆBLESKIVER

Considering three of the three main ingredients—flour, eggs, and milk—are substituted in this recipe, the result is notably close to the classic. Having tested many egg alternatives, I found applesauce, sweetened or unsweetened, to work especially well. The sweetened is more neutral in flavor, while unsweetened adds a little bit of tartness, but either one works well. If you have a different favorite substitute, feel free to exchange the applesauce for the equivalent of two eggs. Similarly, a plant-based butter results in æbleskiver closest to the classic, but any plant-based cooking oil can be used in its place. The sugar is optional but will add only a little bit of sweetness. Even for savory combinations, a dash of sugar will enhance and balance the flavors.

Makes 21 æbleskiver | GF | V

1¼ cups (175 g) sweet rice flour

½ cup (70 g) brown rice flour

½ cup (90 g) potato starch

¼ cup (30 g) tapioca starch

2 tablespoons psyllium husk

1 teaspoon guar gum

1 tablespoon baking powder

½ teaspoon salt

2 tablespoons sugar (optional)

2 cups (480 ml) plant milk

½ cup (120 g) applesauce

2 tablespoons melted plant-based butter + more for the pan

Combine the sweet rice flour, brown rice flour, potato starch, tapioca starch, psyllium husk, guar gum, baking powder, salt, and sugar (if using) in a medium bowl and mix well. Set aside.

In a separate bowl, lightly mix together the plant milk, applesauce, and 2 tablespoons of melted plant-based butter with a fork. Pour the mixture over the dry ingredients and whisk quickly, until just combined. Try not to stir the batter again after this.

Heat the æbleskiver pan over low to medium heat with about ½ teaspoon of melted plant-based butter in each cavity. Using an ice cream scoop or a spoon, fill each cavity almost to the top.

Cook until a crust forms on the batter. Using a thin wooden skewer, turn the æbleskiver 90°, letting the batter spill over. Once a skin has formed, the æbleskiver will turn easily. Turn again in a different direction and then a last time to close up the sphere. Spin the æbleskiver around until evenly golden brown and cooked all the way through. Serve right away or keep the æbleskiver warm in a 200°F (100°C) oven.

PALEO ÆBLESKIVER

Almond flour is a common staple in the paleo kitchen, and with the addition of a couple of extra eggs, it makes a delicious æbleskiver high in protein and good fats. The coconut palm sugar is optional but will add only a little bit of sweetness. Raw honey or maple syrup are also paleo-friendly sugar substitutes. Even for savory combinations, a dash of sugar will enhance and balance the flavors.

Makes 21 æbleskiver | GF

3 cups (270 g) almond flour

½ cup (80 g) tapioca starch

2 tablespoons coconut palm sugar (optional)

½ teaspoon baking soda

½ teaspoon salt

5 large eggs

1 cup (240 ml) almond milk

½ teaspoon vanilla extract

2 tablespoons melted ghee or butter + more for the pan

Combine the almond flour, tapioca starch, coconut palm sugar (if used), baking soda, and salt in a medium bowl and mix. Set aside.

In a separate bowl, lightly mix together the eggs, almond milk, vanilla, and 2 tablespoons of melted ghee with a fork. Pour the mixture over the dry ingredients and whisk quickly, until just combined. Try not to stir the batter again after this.

Heat the æbleskiver pan over low to medium heat with about ½ teaspoon of melted ghee in each cavity. Using an ice cream scoop or a spoon, fill each cavity almost to the top.

Cook until a crust forms on the batter. Using a thin wooden skewer, turn the æbleskiver 90°, letting the batter spill over. Once a skin has formed, the æbleskiver will turn easily. Turn again in a different direction and then a last time to close up the sphere. Spin the æbleskiver around until evenly golden brown and cooked all the way through. Serve right away or keep the æbleskiver warm in a 200°F (100°C) oven.

KETO ÆBLESKIVER

Creamy and light, this keto-friendly æbleskiver has hints of a delicate soufflé. For it to turn smoothly, it cooks at a slightly higher temperature than the classic, and it's important to lift and turn as opposed to push and turn like in most other æbleskiver recipes. Adding sweetener is optional but won't make it notably sweet. Even for savory combinations, a hint of sweetener will enhance and balance the flavors.

Makes 21 æbleskiver | GF

2 cups (180 g) almond flour

2 tablespoons psyllium husk

1 tablespoon baking powder

1 teaspoon guar gum

½ teaspoon salt

5 large eggs

1 cup (215 g) cream cheese

3 tablespoons allulose or other keto-friendly sweetener (optional)

½ cup (120 ml) heavy cream

½ cup (120 ml) water

Ghee or butter for the pan

Combine the almond flour, psyllium husk, baking powder, guar gum, and salt in a medium bowl and mix. Set aside.

In a separate bowl, whisk together the eggs, cream cheese, and allulose (if using) until smooth. Stir in the cream and water and mix until smooth. Pour the mixture over the dry ingredients and whisk quickly, until just combined. Try not to stir the batter again after this.

Heat the æbleskiver pan over medium heat with about ½ teaspoon of ghee in each cavity. Using an ice cream scoop or a spoon, fill each cavity almost to the top.

Cook until a crust forms on the batter. Using a thin wooden skewer, carefully turn the æbleskiver 90° by lifting and rotating, letting the batter spill over. Turn again in a different direction and then a last time to close up the sphere. Spin the æbleskiver around until evenly golden brown and cooked all the way through. Serve right away or keep the æbleskiver warm in a 200°F (100°C) oven.

YEAST ÆBLESKIVER

Best described as somewhere between a pancake and a bread bun, yeast æbleskiver are versatile but, most importantly, incredibly tasty. Serve as regular æbleskiver, as a side dish, or as bread buns. Cut the leftovers in half, toast them in a 350°F (175°C) oven for 4 to 6 minutes, or until the edges turn golden brown and crispy, and serve them slathered with butter (plant-based with the vegan version) and jam.

Using instant yeast, this recipe is as easy as any of the other basic recipes, but remember to add an hour of resting time to the total cooking time.

Each recipe makes about 21 æbleskiver

GLUTEN-FREE YEAST ÆBLESKIVER
GF | NF | VG

1 cup (140 g) sweet rice flour
½ cup (70 g) brown rice flour
½ cup (90 g) potato starch
¼ cup (30 g) tapioca starch
2 tablespoons buttermilk powder
2 tablespoons psyllium husk
1 teaspoon guar gum
½ teaspoon salt
2 tablespoons sugar (optional)
2½ teaspoons instant yeast
1½ cups (360 ml) milk
2 large eggs
Butter for the pan

CLASSIC YEAST ÆBLESKIVER | NF | VG

2¼ cups (315 g) all-purpose flour
2½ teaspoons instant yeast
½ teaspoon salt
2 tablespoons sugar (optional)
1½ cups (360 ml) milk
2 large eggs
Butter for the pan

VEGAN YEAST ÆBLESKIVER | NF | V

2½ cups (350 g) all-purpose flour
1 tablespoon flaxseed meal
2½ teaspoons instant yeast
½ teaspoon salt
2 tablespoons sugar (optional)
1½ cups (360 ml) plant-based milk
½ cup (120 g) applesauce
Plant-based butter for the pan

TO MAKE EACH ÆBLESKIVER: Combine all the dry ingredients in a medium bowl and mix well. Set aside.

In a pan on the stove or in a microwave-safe bowl, heat the milk, or plant-based milk, to a lukewarm temperature. It should be neither hot nor cold to the touch. Lightly mix in the eggs, or the applesauce, and pour the mixture over the dry ingredients. Stir until combined.

Cover the bowl with a clean towel and leave in a warm spot for 1 hour until bubbly and about 50 percent risen.

Gently stir the batter once. Heat the æbleskiver pan over low to medium heat with about ½ teaspoon of butter in each cavity. Using an ice cream scoop or a spoon, fill each cavity almost to the top.

Cook until a crust forms on the batter. Using a thin wooden skewer, turn the æbleskiver 90°, letting the batter spill over. Once a skin has formed, the æbleskiver will turn easily. Turn again in a different direction and then a last time to close up the sphere. Spin the æbleskiver around until evenly golden brown and cooked all the way through. Serve right away or keep the æbleskiver warm in a 200°F (100°C) oven.

GLUTEN-FREE   CLASSIC   VEGAN

SWEET
ÆBLESKIVER

ROASTED APRICOT Æbleskiver with Strawberry Jam   27

RASPBERRY TOSCA Æbleskiver with Caramel and
Sliced Almonds   28

MASCARPONE PEACH Æbleskiver with Vanilla Syrup   31

COCONUT and **PINEAPPLE** Æbleskiver   32

PASSION FRUIT CURD Æbleskiver with Cream Cheese Dip   35

SESAME BANANA Æbleskiver with Honey Ice Cream
and Caramelized Almonds   36

APPLE ALMOND Æbleskiver with Salted Caramel
and Mini Caramel Apples   39

SOURDOUGH Æbleskiver with Roasted Grapes
and Candied Walnuts   42

CITRUS and **POPPYSEED** Æbleskiver with Candied Kumquats in
Citrus Syrup   47

FIG and **PISTACHIO** Æbleskiver with Pistachio Cardamom
Ice Cream   48

PEANUT and **DATE** Æbleskiver with Peanut Chocolate Mousse   51

ALMOND and **RASPBERRY** Æbleskiver with Matcha Glaze   52

CARROT PECAN Æbleskiver with Cream Cheese Custard
and Caramel Drizzle   55

BLUEBERRY CORNBREAD Æbleskiver with Blueberry Syrup   56

ALMOND Æbleskiver with Warm Mixed Berry Compote   59

OAT, GINGER, and **PISTACHIO** Æbleskiver with
Elderflower Glaze   60

WHITE CHOCOLATE HAZELNUT Æbleskiver with
Sweet Beet Ice Cream and Candied Beet Chips   63

CINNAMON RICE Æbleskiver with Risalamalta and Strawberry Syrup   67

BLUE CORN Æbleskiver Skewers with Citrus and Berry Buttercream   68

CHERRY-STUFFED Æbleskiver with Homemade Almond Paste   71

GINGERBREAD Æbleskiver with Lingonberry Cream and Honey Glaze   72

RHUBARB CRUMBLE Æbleskiver with Candied Rhubarb and Ice Cream   75

RED CURRANT HIBISCUS Æbleskiver with Caramel Jam and Zabaglione   77

BLUEBERRY WHOLE-WHEAT Æbleskiver with Blueberry Jam and Whipped Lavender Cream   81

SWEET SAFFRON Æbleskiver with Blueberry–Black Currant Jam   82

CHOCOLATE TRUFFLE Æbleskiver with Chocolate Glaze   85

BUTTERSCOTCH MIDSUMMER WREATH with Whipped Cream and Fresh Berries   86

COFFEE CRUMBLE Æbleskiver with Walnuts and Sweet Espresso Dip   89

WILD STRAWBERRY Æbleskiver with Strawberry Curd and Glaze   90

CHOCOLATE AND BACON Æbleskiver with Spicy Chocolate Glaze   93

CHOCOLATE CARAMEL Æbleskiver with Rum-Raisin Caramel Ice Cream   94

CRUNCHY CINNAMON Æbleskiver with Dark Chocolate Dipping Sauce   97

CHOCOLATE COCONUT Æbleskiver and Chocolate Sauce with a Hint of Mint   98

ZEBRA Æbleskiver with Chocolate Marble Sauce   101

CHOCOLATE LAVA Æbleskiver with Whipped Cream and Gold Leaf   102

ROASTED APRICOT ÆBLESKIVER
WITH STRAWBERRY JAM

Makes about 14 æbleskiver | NF | VG

STRAWBERRY JAM

2 pounds (910 g) fresh strawberries, hulled + more for serving

1½ cups (300 g) sugar

Zest and juice from 1 lemon

ÆBLESKIVER

2 pounds (910 g) fresh apricots, pitted and cut into quarters + more for serving

1 cup (200 g) sugar

Juice from 1 lemon

1½ cups (210 g) all-purpose flour

1 tablespoon baking powder

½ teaspoon salt

2 large eggs

2 cups (480 ml) milk or buttermilk

2 tablespoons melted butter + more for the pan

½ cup (120 g) Strawberry Jam (above) or store-bought

TO MAKE THE JAM: Wash the strawberries and dry completely. In a large pot, combine the berries, sugar, lemon zest, and lemon juice.

Cook over medium-high heat, stirring occasionally, until the juice thickens to a light syrup, about 15 minutes. If there is a lot of foam on the surface, skim it off with a spoon or spatula.

Leftover strawberry jam can be stored in an airtight container and refrigerated for up to 4 weeks.

TO MAKE THE ÆBLESKIVER: Preheat the oven to 350°F (175°C).

Place the apricots snugly, skin side down, in a 9-by-12-inch (23-by-30-cm) baking dish. Sprinkle with the sugar and lemon juice. Roast for 30 minutes, or until the apricots start to caramelize. Remove from the oven and let the apricots cool in the baking dish. Leftover apricots can be stored in an airtight container and refrigerated for up to 4 weeks.

Combine the flour, baking powder, and salt in a large bowl and mix well. Set aside.

In a separate bowl, mix together the eggs, milk, and 2 tablespoons of butter. Pour the mixture over the dry ingredients and stir quickly until just combined. Gently fold in 1 cup (140 g) of the apricots, leaving any big chunks as is. Try not to stir the batter again after this.

Heat the æbleskiver pan over low to medium heat with ½ to 1 teaspoon of butter in each cavity. Once the butter starts to bubble, use an ice cream scoop or a spoon to drop a dollop of batter into each cavity. Spoon 1 to 1½ teaspoons of the strawberry jam on top. Cover each cavity with more batter. Don't worry if a bit of filling leaks out.

Cook until a crust forms on the batter. Use a thin wooden skewer to turn the æbleskiver 90°, letting the batter spill over. Turn again in a different direction and then a last time to close up the sphere. Spin the æbleskiver around until evenly golden brown and a toothpick inserted into it comes out mostly clean. Serve right away or keep the æbleskiver warm in a 200°F (100°C) oven.

TO SERVE: Serve the æbleskiver with fresh strawberries and apricots and generous amounts of jam.

RASPBERRY TOSCA ÆBLESKIVER
WITH CARAMEL AND SLICED ALMONDS

Makes about 14 æbleskiver | VG

TOSCA CARAMEL WITH ALMONDS

1 cup (220 g) butter

½ cup (100 g) sugar

¼ cup (35 g) all-purpose flour

¼ cup (60 ml) milk

6 ounces (170 g) sliced almonds

ÆBLESKIVER

2 cups (240 g) fresh raspberries

¾ cup (150 g) sugar

2 large eggs

1½ cups (210 g) all-purpose flour

1 tablespoon baking powder

½ teaspoon salt

1 cup (240 ml) milk

½ cup (120 ml) heavy cream

½ cup (110 g) melted butter + more for the pan

TO MAKE THE TOSCA CARAMEL: Combine the butter, sugar, flour, and milk in a small pan over low heat. Cook, stirring often, until the mixture is thick and slightly darker, about 5 minutes. Stir in the almonds and simmer for another couple of minutes. Remove from the heat and set aside.

TO MAKE THE ÆBLESKIVER: Preheat the oven to 350°F (180°C).

Mash the raspberries with a fork in a small pan over medium-low heat. Add ¼ cup (50 g) of the sugar and cook, stirring, until the sugar has melted and the mixture thickens. Remove from the heat and set aside.

Using an electric mixer, beat the eggs and the remaining ½ cup (100 g) of sugar in a large bowl on high speed until white and fluffy. Lower the mixer speed to medium and add the flour, baking powder, salt, milk, cream, and ½ cup (110 g) of melted butter and beat until incorporated.

Heat the æbleskiver pan over low to medium heat with ½ to 1 teaspoon of butter in each cavity. Once the butter starts to bubble, use an ice cream scoop or a spoon to drop a dollop of batter into each cavity. Spoon 1 to 1½ teaspoons of the mashed raspberries on top. Cover each cavity with more batter. Don't worry if a bit of filling leaks out.

Cook until a crust forms on the batter. Use a thin wooden skewer to turn the æbleskiver 90°, letting the batter spill over. Turn again in a different direction and then a last time to close up the sphere. Spin the æbleskiver around until evenly golden brown and a toothpick inserted into it comes out mostly clean.

Butter a 9-by-13-inch (23-by-33-cm) baking dish or similar size oven-safe pan. Place the æbleskiver close together in the pan. Spoon the tosca caramel over the æbleskiver. Bake for 10 to 15 minutes, or until the almonds are lightly toasted and the caramel is golden brown.

TO SERVE: Serve the æbleskiver right away or keep the æbleskiver warm in a 200°F (100°C) oven.

MASCARPONE PEACH ÆBLESKIVER
WITH VANILLA SYRUP

Makes about 21 æbleskiver | NF | VG

MASCARPONE

**2 cups (480 ml) heavy cream
(not ultra-pasteurized and
preferably raw)**

**1 tablespoon fresh lemon juice
(or ⅛ teaspoon tartaric acid)**

VANILLA SYRUP

2 cups (480 ml) water

2 cups (400 g) sugar

**¼ teaspoon pure vanilla powder or
the seeds of 1 vanilla bean**

ÆBLESKIVER

5 fresh peaches

**2 tablespoons butter + more for
the pan**

½ cup (100 g) sugar

**¼ teaspoon pure vanilla powder
or the seeds of 1 vanilla bean**

1 tablespoon fresh lemon juice

1½ cups (210 g) all-purpose flour

2 teaspoons baking powder

½ teaspoon baking soda

½ teaspoon salt

1½ cups (360 ml) milk

**4 ounces (115 g) Mascarpone
(above) or store-bought**

1 egg

Zest of 1 lemon

TO MAKE THE MASCARPONE: Heat the cream in a saucepan over medium heat until it reaches 190°F (85°C). Keep the temperature steady for 5 minutes. Add the lemon juice and stir for 1 minute, or until the cream curdles. Pour the curdled cream into a colander lined with cheesecloth and let drain over a bowl in the refrigerator for at least 12 and up to 24 hours. If the mascarpone is too dry, stir some of the whey back in. To store, refrigerate in an airtight container for up to 4 days.

TO MAKE THE SYRUP: In a saucepan, combine the water, sugar, and vanilla. Bring to a boil over medium-high heat, stirring often, until the sugar dissolves. Continue to boil without stirring until the syrup thickens slightly, 2 to 3 minutes. Remove from the heat and let cool. Pour the syrup into a jar with a tight-fitting lid. The syrup can be stored in the refrigerator for up to 2 weeks.

TO MAKE THE ÆBLESKIVER: Cut 3 of the peaches into cubes. Melt the butter in a small pan over medium heat. Add the sugar, vanilla, lemon juice, and cubed peaches and cook, stirring often, until some of the liquid has evaporated and it becomes a thick, chunky paste, 10 to 15 minutes. Remove from the heat and let cool to room temperature.

In a large bowl, combine the flour, baking powder, baking soda, and salt and mix well. In a separate bowl, combine the milk, mascarpone, egg, and lemon zest and beat with an electric mixer until smooth. Pour the mixture over the dry ingredients and stir until just incorporated. Gently stir in the peach mixture. Try not to stir the batter again after this.

Heat the æbleskiver pan over low to medium heat with about ½ teaspoon of butter in each cavity. Using an ice cream scoop or a spoon, fill each cavity almost to the top.

Cook until a crust forms on the batter. Using a thin wooden skewer, turn the æbleskiver 90°, letting the batter spill over. Once a skin has formed, the æbleskiver will turn easily. Turn again in a different direction and then a last time to close up the sphere. Spin the æbleskiver around until evenly golden brown and cooked all the way through. Serve right away or keep the æbleskiver warm in a 200°F (100°C) oven.

TO SERVE: Drizzle a little syrup over the pancakes. Cut the remaining 2 fresh peaches into wedges and serve with the rest of the syrup.

COCONUT AND PINEAPPLE ÆBLESKIVER

Makes about 14 æbleskiver | NF | VG

1 cup (60 g) sweetened shredded coconut

¼ cup (55 g) melted butter + more for the pan

2 large eggs

2 cups (280 g) chopped fresh, frozen, or canned pineapple, drained

1 cup (240 ml) milk

½ cup (120 ml) heavy cream

1½ cups (210 g) all-purpose flour

1 tablespoon baking powder

½ teaspoon salt

½ cup (40 g) large coconut flakes, for serving

In a medium bowl, stir together the shredded coconut, ¼ cup (55 g) of melted butter, and eggs. Set aside.

In another bowl, mix together 1 cup (140 g) of the pineapple, the milk, and cream until well combined. Set aside.

In a third large bowl, combine the flour, baking powder, and salt and mix together. Pour in the pineapple mixture and then the coconut mixture and stir quickly until just combined. Try not to stir the batter again after this.

Heat the æbleskiver pan over low to medium heat with about ½ teaspoon of butter in each cavity. Using an ice cream scoop or a spoon, fill each cavity almost to the top.

Cook until a crust forms on the batter. Using a thin wooden skewer, turn the æbleskiver 90°, letting the batter spill over. Once a skin has formed, the æbleskiver will turn easily. Turn again in a different direction and then a last time to close up the sphere. Spin the æbleskiver around until evenly golden brown and cooked all the way through. Serve right away or keep the æbleskiver warm in a 200°F (100°C) oven.

TO SERVE: Serve the æbleskiver with the remaining 1 cup (140 g) of fresh pineapple and the large coconut flakes.

PASSION FRUIT CURD ÆBLESKIVER
WITH CREAM CHEESE DIP

Makes about 21 æbleskiver | NF | VG

PASSION FRUIT CURD

Pulp and juice from 6 passion fruits

¾ cup (150 g) granulated sugar

4 large egg yolks

½ cup (110 g) butter, cubed

CREAM CHEESE DIP

4 ounces (115 g) cream cheese

¾ cup (180 ml) heavy whipping cream

½ cup (60 g) powdered sugar

ÆBLESKIVER

2 cups (280 g) all-purpose flour

1 tablespoon baking powder

½ teaspoon salt

½ cup (130 g) Passion Fruit Curd (above) or store-bought

4 ounces (115 g) cream cheese

1¼ cups (300 ml) milk

2 large eggs

2 tablespoons melted butter + more for the pan

TO MAKE THE PASSION FRUIT CURD: If you prefer a curd without seeds, strain the pulp through a fine-mesh sieve to remove them.

In a medium saucepan over medium-low heat, whisk together the granulated sugar and egg yolks until light and fluffy. Stir in the passion fruit pulp and juice. Cook, whisking constantly, until the mixture thickens.

Remove from the heat and stir in the cubed butter until melted and incorporated. Transfer the curd to an airtight container and refrigerate. The curd can be stored in the refrigerator for up to 1 week.

TO MAKE THE CREAM CHEESE DIP: Using an electric mixer, whisk the cream cheese in a bowl until soft. Add the heavy cream, a little at a time, and continue to whisk until soft peaks form. Add the powdered sugar and whisk until smooth. Store the dip in an airtight container in the refrigerator for up to 1 week.

TO MAKE THE ÆBLESKIVER: In a large bowl, mix the flour, baking powder, and salt. Set aside.

In another bowl, stir together the ½ cup (130 g) of passion fruit curd and the cream cheese to make a soft cream. Set aside.

In a third bowl, lightly stir together the milk, eggs, and 2 tablespoons of melted butter until combined. Pour the mixture over the dry ingredients and stir quickly until just combined.

Gently fold in the cream cheese curd mixture and try not to stir the batter again after this.

Heat the æbleskiver pan over low to medium heat with about ½ teaspoon of butter in each cavity. Using an ice cream scoop or a spoon, fill each cavity almost to the top.

Cook until a crust forms on the batter. Using a thin wooden skewer, turn the æbleskiver 90°, letting the batter spill over. Once a skin has formed, the æbleskiver will turn easily. Turn again in a different direction and then a last time to close up the sphere. Spin the æbleskiver around until evenly golden brown and cooked all the way through. Serve right away or keep the æbleskiver warm in a 200°F (100°C) oven.

TO SERVE: Serve the æbleskiver topped with a moderate amount of the remaining curd and the cream cheese dip and serve more on the side.

SESAME BANANA ÆBLESKIVER
WITH HONEY ICE CREAM AND CARAMELIZED ALMONDS

Makes about 21 æbleskiver | VG

HONEY ICE CREAM

4 egg yolks

2 tablespoons honey

2 cups (480 ml) heavy whipping cream

Seeds from 1 vanilla bean

CARAMELIZED MARCONA ALMONDS

8 ounces (230 g) roasted and salted Marcona almonds

2 tablespoons honey

2 tablespoons sesame seeds

CONTINUED

TO MAKE THE ICE CREAM: In a saucepan over low heat, beat together the egg yolks and honey until light and fluffy. Stir in 1 cup (240 ml) of the heavy cream and heat slowly while continually stirring until the custard thickens enough to forms a film over the back of a spoon. Do not boil or the custard will curdle. Let cool and then refrigerate until the custard is cold, 1 to 2 hours.

In a medium bowl, combine the remaining 1 cup (240 ml) of heavy cream with the vanilla bean seeds and beat on high speed until soft peaks form. Whisk in the cooled custard. Pour the mixture into a 9-by-5-inch (23-by-12-cm) loaf pan or another similar size freezer-safe container. Cover and place in the freezer for 1 hour.

Remove the ice cream from the freezer and whip it with an electric mixer for a few minutes. Repeat every hour for the next 2 to 3 hours. Freeze overnight before serving.

TO MAKE THE ALMONDS: Preheat the oven to 350°F (180°C). Line a baking sheet with parchment paper.

Combine all the ingredients in a saucepan over medium heat and cook, stirring, just until the almonds are coated with honey and sesame seeds.

Spread the nuts in a single layer on the prepared baking sheet. Bake for 10 to 15 minutes, or until golden. Let the nuts cool before breaking them apart. Store in an airtight container at room temperature for up to 3 weeks.

CONTINUED

SESAME BANANA ÆBLESKIVER
CONTINUED

ÆBLESKIVER

5 tablespoons melted butter + more for the pan

¼ cup (50 g) brown sugar

¼ cup (85 g) honey + more for serving

6 medium ripe bananas, sliced and tossed with 1 tablespoon fresh lemon juice

1½ cups (210 g) all-purpose flour

3 tablespoons granulated sugar

2 teaspoons baking powder

½ teaspoon salt

1¼ cups (300 ml) milk

2 large eggs

2 tablespoons sesame seeds

TO MAKE THE ÆBLESKIVER: Pour 3 tablespoons of the butter into a frying pan and place over medium heat. Add the brown sugar and honey and stir just until the sugar has melted into a caramel, about 2 minutes.

Add the sliced bananas and stir continuously until the caramel thickens slightly, 2 to 3 minutes. Remove the pan from the heat. Use two-thirds of the bananas for the batter and save the rest for serving.

In a large bowl, stir together the flour, granulated sugar, baking powder, and salt. Set aside.

In a medium bowl, lightly mix together the milk, eggs, and remaining 2 tablespoons of melted butter. Pour the mixture over the dry ingredients and stir quickly until just combined.

Gently fold in the caramelized bananas and try not to stir the batter again after this.

Heat the æbleskiver pan over low to medium heat with about ½ teaspoon of butter in each cavity. Sprinkle ⅛ to ¼ teaspoon sesame seeds over the melted butter before using an ice cream scoop or a spoon to fill each cavity almost to the top.

Cook until a crust forms on the batter. Using a thin wooden skewer, turn the æbleskiver 90°, letting the batter spill over. Once a skin has formed, the æbleskiver will turn easily. Turn again in a different direction and then a last time to close up the sphere. Spin the æbleskiver around until evenly golden brown and cooked all the way through. Serve right away or keep the æbleskiver warm in a 200°F (100°C) oven.

TO SERVE: Accompany the æbleskiver with scoops of the honey ice cream drizzled with honey, caramelized bananas, and a scattering of caramelized Marcona almonds.

APPLE ALMOND ÆBLESKIVER
WITH SALTED CARAMEL AND MINI CARAMEL APPLES

Makes about 21 æbleskiver | VG

SALTED CARAMEL

½ cup (120 ml) water

1 cup (200 g) granulated sugar

½ cup (100 g) dark brown sugar

½ teaspoon salt

¼ cup (55 g) butter

½ cup (120 ml) heavy whipping cream

MINI CARAMEL APPLES

Fourteen 1- to 1½-inch (2.5- to 4-cm) mini apples

Fourteen 4½-inch (11-cm) wooden skewers

½ cup (110 g) butter

1 cup (200 g) light brown sugar

1 cup (240 ml) light corn syrup

¾ cup (180 ml) heavy whipping cream

½ cup (60 g) chopped almonds

CONTINUED

TO MAKE THE SALTED CARAMEL: In a medium saucepan over medium-low heat, combine the water, granulated sugar, brown sugar, and salt and cook, stirring often, until the sugar dissolves. Add the butter and continue to cook, stirring, until the butter has melted.

Stop stirring at this point. Let the caramel cook until it changes color to a deep amber, about 15 minutes. Watch closely to avoid burning. Remove the pan from the heat. Stir in the cream. Set aside.

The salted caramel can be refrigerated in an airtight container for up to 4 weeks. It will harden as it cools but softens when reheated.

TO MAKE THE CARAMEL APPLES: Line a baking sheet with parchment paper.

Wash and dry the apples thoroughly. Place a skewer into the bottom of each apple, but not all the way through. Store in the refrigerator.

In a medium saucepan over medium-low heat, combine the butter, brown sugar, corn syrup, and cream and cook, stirring often, until the butter has melted. Bring to a boil and cook until the temperature reaches 240°F (115°C) on a candy thermometer. Remove from the heat and let the caramel cool until it's thick enough to coat the apples, about 15 minutes.

Dip the skewered apples in the caramel, then roll them in the chopped almonds. Place them standing on the prepared baking sheet and refrigerate until ready to serve.

CONTINUED

APPLE ALMOND ÆBLESKIVER
CONTINUED

ÆBLESKIVER

¼ cup (55 g) butter + more for the pan

1 large apple, peeled and thinly sliced

¼ cup (50 g) light brown sugar

½ cup (60 g) chopped almonds

1½ cups (210 g) all-purpose flour

1 tablespoon ground cinnamon

1 tablespoon baking powder

½ teaspoon salt

2 large eggs

1½ cups (360 ml) milk

TO MAKE THE ÆBLESKIVER: Melt the ¼ cup (55 g) of butter in a frying pan over medium heat and add the sliced apple. Cook for 5 minutes, stirring occasionally. Add the brown sugar, stir until melted, and continue to cook until the liquid thickens, about 5 minutes. Take off the heat, stir in ¼ cup (30 g) of the chopped almonds, and set aside.

Combine the flour, cinnamon, baking powder, and salt in a large bowl, and then stir in the eggs and milk until just blended.

Gently fold in the apple caramel and try not to stir the batter after this.

Heat the æbleskiver pan over low to medium heat with about ½ teaspoon of butter in each cavity. Using an ice cream scoop or a spoon, fill each cavity almost to the top.

Cook until a crust forms on the batter. Using a thin wooden skewer, turn the æbleskiver 90°, letting the batter spill over. Once a skin has formed, the æbleskiver will turn easily. Turn again in a different direction and then a last time to close up the sphere. Spin the æbleskiver around until evenly golden brown and a toothpick inserted into it comes out mostly clean. Serve right away or keep the æbleskiver warm in a 200°F (100°C) oven.

TO SERVE: Serve the æbleskiver warm topped with the salted caramel and the remaining ¼ cup (30 g) chopped almonds and a side of caramel apples.

SOURDOUGH ÆBLESKIVER
WITH ROASTED GRAPES AND CANDIED WALNUTS

Makes about 21 æbleskiver | VG

1 cup (225 g) sourdough starter

2½ cups (300 g) all-purpose flour

2 cups (475 ml) milk

2 tablespoons sugar

1 teaspoon baking powder

½ teaspoon salt

2 large eggs

½ cup roasted grapes

Butter for the pan

Combine the sourdough starter, flour, milk, and sugar in a medium bowl and mix well. Cover with a clean towel and leave on the counter overnight, 8 to 10 hours.

Add the baking powder, salt, eggs, and roasted grapes, and stir until combined.

Heat the æbleskiver pan over low to medium heat with about ½ teaspoon of butter in each cavity. Using an ice cream scoop or a spoon, fill each cavity almost to the top.

Cook until a crust forms on the batter. Using a thin wooden skewer, turn the æbleskiver 90°, letting the batter spill over. Once a skin has formed, the æbleskiver will turn easily. Turn again in a different direction and then a last time to close up the sphere. Spin the æbleskiver around until evenly golden brown and cooked all the way through. Serve right away with candied walnuts scattered over the top, or keep the aebleskiver warm in a 200°F (100°C) oven.

ROASTED GRAPES

Makes about 3 cups (450 g) | GF | NF | V

2 pounds (910 g) grapes
2 tablespoons grapeseed oil
¼ teaspoon salt

Preheat the oven to 400°F (200°C).

Spread the grapes on a baking sheet. Drizzle with the grapeseed oil and sprinkle with the salt. Toss the grapes to evenly coat.

Bake for 7 to 20 minutes, depending on the size of the grapes, until they are beginning to blister. Remove from the oven and let cool.

VARIATION: Roasted Grapes in Syrup

- If you like you can strain the grapes through a cheesecloth and reserve the pure grape syrup for another use.

- Or add some liqueur or fresh herbs to the roasted grapes to change the flavor profile.

CANDIED WALNUTS

Makes about 1½ cups (180 g) | GF | VG

1½ cups (280 g) walnuts
¼ cup (50 g) sugar
¼ cup (60 ml) maple syrup
2 tablespoons butter
¼ teaspoon salt

Preheat the oven to 350°F (180°C). Line a baking sheet with parchment paper.

Toss all the ingredients in a bowl until the nuts are evenly coated.

Spread the mixture evenly on the prepared baking sheet. Bake, turning the pan halfway through, until fragrant and golden brown, 5 to 10 minutes.

Store in an airtight container in the refrigerator for up to 1 week.

CITRUS AND POPPY SEED ÆBLESKIVER
WITH CANDIED KUMQUATS IN CITRUS SYRUP

Makes about 14 æbleskiver | NF | VG

CANDIED KUMQUATS IN CITRUS SYRUP

2 cups (400 g) kumquats

1 cup (240 ml) orange juice

Juice from 1 lemon

1½ cups (300 g) sugar

ÆBLESKIVER

1½ cups (210 g) all-purpose flour

1 tablespoon baking powder

½ teaspoon salt

2 cups (480 ml) buttermilk

2 large eggs

½ cup (100 g) Candied Kumquats (above)

2 tablespoons poppy seeds

2 tablespoons melted butter + more for the pan

TO MAKE THE CANDIED KUMQUATS: Preheat the oven to 200°F (100°C). Line a baking sheet with parchment paper.

Leave the smallest kumquats whole and cut the rest into thin slices.

In a saucepan, bring the orange juice, lemon juice, and sugar to a boil over medium heat. Add all the kumquats to the liquid and simmer for 30-40 minutes until it turns into a bubbly syrup.

Remove the kumquats with a slotted spoon and spread them evenly on the prepared baking sheet. Bake for 1 hour, until the kumquats are dried and candied.

Store the kumquats in a jar with a lid and cover with the syrup. Refrigerate for up to 3 weeks. Makes about 1½ cups (500 g).

TO MAKE THE ÆBLESKIVER: Combine the flour, baking powder, and salt in a large bowl and mix well. Set aside.

In a medium bowl, lightly mix together the buttermilk, eggs, candied kumquats, poppy seeds, and 2 tablespoons of melted butter. Pour the mixture over the dry ingredients and stir until just combined. Try not to stir the batter again after this.

Heat the æbleskiver pan over low to medium heat with about ½ teaspoon of butter in each cavity. Using an ice cream scoop or a spoon, fill each cavity almost to the top.

Cook until a crust forms on the batter. Using a thin wooden skewer, turn the æbleskiver 90°, letting the batter spill over. Once a skin has formed, the æbleskiver will turn easily. Turn again in a different direction and then a last time to close up the sphere. Spin the æbleskiver around until evenly golden brown and cooked all the way through. Serve right away or keep the æbleskiver warm in a 200°F (100°C) oven.

TO SERVE: Serve the æbleskiver with the candied kumquats in citrus syrup.

FIG AND PISTACHIO ÆBLESKIVER
WITH PISTACHIO CARDAMOM ICE CREAM

Makes about 21 æbleskiver | VG

PISTACHIO CARDAMOM ICE CREAM

8 ounces (230 g) farmer's cheese

1 cup (200 g) sugar

1 teaspoon ground cardamom

2 cups (480 ml) heavy whipping cream

½ cup (60 g) chopped pistachios

PISTACHIO FIG PASTE

5 ounces (140 g) dried figs

7 ounces (200 g) roasted salted pistachio nuts

½ cup (120 ml) maple syrup

1 tablespoon fresh lemon juice

ÆBLESKIVER

2 cups (280 g) all-purpose flour

1 tablespoon baking powder

½ teaspoon salt

1 teaspoon ground cardamom (optional)

½ cup (60 g) chopped pistachios + more for serving

2 cups (480 ml) milk

2 large eggs

¼ cup (60 ml) maple syrup

¼ cup (55 g) melted butter + more for the pan

½ cup (120 g) Pistachio Fig Paste (above)

Fresh figs, for serving

Chopped pistachios, for serving

TO MAKE THE ICE CREAM: In a stand mixer, combine the farmer's cheese, sugar, and cardamom and mix until smooth. Transfer to a bowl and clean out the stand mixer.

In the stand mixer, whisk the cream until firm peaks form.

Gently fold the whipped cream into the farmer's cheese mixture. Fold in the pistachios. Pour the mixture into a 9-by-5-inch (23-by-12-cm) loaf pan. Cover and freeze for at least 4 hours or overnight.

TO MAKE THE FIG PASTE: Trim any hard stems off the figs and discard them. Coarsely chop the figs. In a bowl, soak the figs and pistachios in lukewarm water for 15 minutes.

Drain and squeeze the figs gently to remove excess liquid, reserving some of the liquid. Combine the figs, pistachios, maple syrup, and lemon juice in a food processor and process until the mixture is smooth. If the mixture doesn't quite hold together, add a bit of the reserved soaking water, 1 tablespoon at a time, until it reaches the desired consistency. Set aside.

TO MAKE THE ÆBLESKIVER: In a large bowl, combine the flour, baking powder, salt, cardamom (if using), and pistachios and mix well. Set aside.

In a separate bowl, mix together the milk, eggs, maple syrup, and ¼ cup (55 g) of melted butter. Pour the mixture over the dry ingredients and whisk quickly until just combined. Try not to stir the batter again after this.

Heat the æbleskiver pan over low to medium heat with ½ to 1 teaspoon of butter in each cavity. Once the butter starts to bubble, use an ice cream scoop or a spoon to drop a dollop of batter into each cavity. Spoon 1 to 1½ teaspoons of pistachio fig paste on top and push it lightly into the batter. Cover each cavity with more batter. Don't worry if a bit of filling leaks out.

Cook until a crust forms on the batter. Using a thin wooden skewer to turn the æbleskiver 90°, letting the batter spill over. Turn again in a different direction and then a last time to close up the sphere. Spin the æbleskiver around until evenly golden brown and a toothpick inserted into it comes out mostly clean. Serve right away or keep the æbleskiver warm in a 200°F (100°C) oven.

TO SERVE: Serve the æbleskiver with the cardamom ice cream, fresh figs, and a sprinkling of chopped pistachios.

PEANUT AND DATE ÆBLESKIVER
WITH PEANUT CHOCOLATE MOUSSE

Makes about 21 large or 42 small (1½ to 1¾-inch/4 to 4.5-cm) æbleskiver | VG

PEANUT CHOCOLATE MOUSSE

2 cups (480 ml) heavy whipping cream

½ cup (100 g) granulated sugar

8 ounces (230 g) semisweet chocolate chips

½ cup (130 g) peanut butter

3 egg yolks

PEANUT BUTTER CREAM

1 cup (260 g) peanut butter

½ cup (60 g) powdered sugar

ÆBLESKIVER

2 cups (280 g) all-purpose flour

1 tablespoon baking powder

½ teaspoon salt

1 cup (180 g) chopped dates + more for serving

½ cup (100 g) brown sugar

2 tablespoons butter + more for the pan

2¾ cups (660 ml) milk

2 large eggs

¼ cup (35 g) chopped roasted salted peanuts, for serving

TO MAKE THE MOUSSE: In a large bowl, whisk 1½ cups (360 ml) of the heavy cream until stiff peaks form. Cover and refrigerate.

In a saucepan over medium heat, combine the granulated sugar with the remaining ½ cup (120 ml) of heavy cream and heat until the liquid starts bubbling around the edges. Remove from the heat, add the chocolate chips and peanut butter, and stir until smooth.

In a separate bowl, add the egg yolks, spoon one-third of the chocolate mixture, and whisk until smooth. Pour the mixture back into the saucepan turn the heat to low, and cook, stirring often, until the mixture is hot but not boiling. Let cool and then refrigerate until cold, at least 1 hour.

Gently stir the chilled peanut-chocolate mixture into the reserved whipped cream until well mixed. Refrigerate until set and ready to serve. The mousse can be stored in the refrigerator in an airtight container for up to 1 week.

TO MAKE THE PEANUT BUTTER CREAM: In a small bowl, combine the peanut butter and powdered sugar. Using an electric mixer, beat until creamy and well combined. Transfer the mixture to a piping bag with a small tip. The peanut butter cream can be stored in the fridge for up to 3 weeks.

TO MAKE THE ÆBLESKIVER: In a large bowl, mix together the flour, baking powder, and salt. Set aside.

In a separate bowl, stir 1 cup (180 g) of the chopped dates, the brown sugar, and 2 tablespoons of melted butter. Add milk and eggs and stir until combined. Pour the mixture over the dry ingredients and stir quickly until just combined. Try not to stir the batter again after this.

Heat the æbleskiver pan over low to medium heat with about ½ teaspoon of butter in each cavity. Use an ice cream scoop or a spoon to fill each cavity almost to the top.

Cook until a crust forms on the batter. Using a thin wooden skewer, turn the æbleskiver 90°, letting the batter spill over. Once a skin has formed, the æbleskiver will turn easily. Turn again in a different direction, and then a last time to close up the sphere. Spin the æbleskiver around until evenly golden brown and cooked all the way through. Serve right away or keep the æbleskiver

TO SERVE: Pipe the mousse directly onto the plates and serve with the æbleskiver, piped with mini swirls of peanut butter cream and a sprinkling of chopped dates and peanuts.

ALMOND AND RASPBERRY ÆBLESKIVER
WITH MATCHA GLAZE

Makes about 21 æbleskiver | VG

MATCHA GLAZE
1½ cups (180 g) powdered sugar
1 teaspoon matcha powder
¼ teaspoon salt
2 to 3 tablespoons milk

ÆBLESKIVER
1 cup (90 g) almond flour
1 cup (140 g) all-purpose flour
1 tablespoon baking powder
¼ cup (50 g) granulated sugar
½ teaspoon salt
2 cups (480 ml) buttermilk
2 large eggs
¼ cup (55 g) melted butter + more for the pan
1 cup (120 g) fresh or frozen raspberries
½ cup (50 g) sliced almonds

3 tablespoons freeze-dried raspberries, for serving

TO MAKE THE GLAZE: In a medium bowl, mix together the powdered sugar, matcha powder, and salt. Add 2 tablespoons of milk and whisk until smooth and pourable. Add more milk, 1 teaspoon at a time, to reach the desired consistency. Don't be tempted to add too much; it gets runny fast.

TO MAKE THE ÆBLESKIVER: In a large bowl, combine the almond flour, all-purpose flour, baking powder, granulated sugar, and salt and mix well. Set aside.

In a medium bowl, mix together the buttermilk, eggs, and ¼ cup (55 g) of melted butter. Pour the mixture over the dry ingredients and stir quickly until just combined. Gently fold in the fresh raspberries and sliced almonds. Try not to stir the batter again after this.

Heat the æbleskiver pan over low to medium heat with about ½ teaspoon of butter in each cavity. Using an ice cream scoop or a spoon, fill each cavity almost to the top.

Cook until a crust forms on the batter. Using a thin wooden skewer, turn the æbleskiver 90°, letting the batter spill over. Once a skin has formed, the æbleskiver will turn easily. Turn again in a different direction and then a last time to close up the sphere. Spin the æbleskiver around until evenly golden brown and cooked all the way through. Serve right away or keep the æbleskiver warm in a 200°F (100°C) oven.

TO SERVE: Place the æbleskiver on plates. Pour the matcha glaze over the top and sprinkle with the freeze-dried raspberries.

CARROT PECAN ÆBLESKIVER
WITH CREAM CHEESE CUSTARD AND CARAMEL DRIZZLE

Makes about 14 large or 28 small (1½ to 1¾-inch/4 to 4.5-cm) æbleskiver | VG

CARAMEL DRIZZLE

½ cup (110 g) butter

1 cup (200 g) light brown sugar

One 14-ounce (400-ml) can sweetened condensed milk

½ cup (120 ml) light corn syrup or agave

ÆBLESKIVER

1 cup (140 g) all-purpose flour

1 tablespoon baking powder

½ teaspoon salt

1 cup (240 ml) milk

1 large egg

½ cup (100 g) light brown sugar

½ cup (60 g) chopped pecans + more for garnish

1 cup (115 g) finely grated carrot

2 tablespoons melted butter + more for the pan

CREAM CHEESE CUSTARD

16 ounces (455 g) cream cheese

½ cup (100 g) granulated sugar

¼ cup (60 g) sour cream

2 large eggs

TO MAKE THE CARAMEL DRIZZLE: In a saucepan over medium heat, combine the butter and brown sugar and cook, stirring, until the sugar has melted. While continuing to stir, mix in the condensed milk and the syrup. Bring to a simmer and cook, stirring often, until the mixture thickens, 5 to 10 minutes. Set aside. Use immediately or store in an airtight container in the refrigerator for up to 2 weeks.

TO MAKE THE ÆBLESKIVER: In a large bowl, add the flour, baking powder, and salt and mix well. Set aside.

In a medium bowl, mix together the milk, egg, brown sugar, pecans, grated carrot, and 2 tablespoons of melted butter. Pour the mixture over the dry ingredients and stir quickly until just combined. Try not to stir the batter again after this.

Heat the æbleskiver pan over low to medium heat with about ½ teaspoon of butter in each cavity. Using an ice cream scoop or a spoon, fill each cavity almost to the top.

Cook until a crust forms on the batter. Using a thin wooden skewer, turn the æbleskiver 90°, letting the batter spill over. Once a skin has formed, the æbleskiver will turn easily. Turn again in a different direction and then a last time to close up the sphere. Spin the æbleskiver around until evenly golden brown and cooked all the way through. Set aside.

TO MAKE THE CUSTARD: Preheat the oven to 300°F (150°C). Butter an 8- to 10-inch (20- to 25-cm) cast-iron frying pan or springform pan.

In a medium bowl, beat the cream cheese with an electric mixer until smooth. Add the granulated sugar and sour cream and mix until incorporated.

In a separate bowl, whisk the eggs with a fork until broken. Using the electric mixer, slowly add the eggs to the cream cheese mixture and whisk until smooth. Pour the mixture into the prepared frying pan. Place the æbleskiver on top and gently push down. Bake for 45 minutes, or until the custard sets.

TO SERVE: Top the æbleskiver with the caramel drizzle and sprinkle with chopped pecans. Enjoy warm or cold.

BLUEBERRY CORNBREAD ÆBLESKIVER
WITH BLUEBERRY SYRUP

Makes about 14 æbleskiver | NF | VG

BLUEBERRY SYRUP

2 cups (280 g) fresh blueberries

1 cup (240 ml) water

1 cup (200 g) sugar

1 tablespoon fresh lemon juice

Zest of 1 lemon

1 tablespoon cornstarch

ÆBLESKIVER

1 cup (240 ml) milk

2 tablespoons fresh lemon juice

½ cup (70 g) all-purpose flour

1 cup (140 g) fine ground yellow cornmeal

½ cup (100 g) sugar

2 teaspoons baking powder

½ teaspoon baking soda

½ teaspoon salt

2 large eggs

3 cups (420 g) fresh blueberries

Zest of 1 lemon

¼ cup (55 g) melted butter + more for the pan

TO MAKE THE BLUEBERRY SYRUP: In a medium saucepan, combine the blueberries, water, sugar, lemon juice, lemon zest, and cornstarch and bring to a boil over medium heat. Decrease the heat to low and simmer until the blueberries burst and the syrup thickens, 5 to 10 minutes.

Strain the mixture through a fine-mesh sieve or strainer. Discard the solids and set the syrup aside for serving.

TO MAKE THE ÆBLESKIVER: Stir together the milk and lemon juice in a small bowl and let sit for a few minutes to thicken.

In a large bowl, combine the flour, cornmeal, sugar, baking powder, baking soda, and salt and mix well.

Add the milk mixture and eggs and whisk quickly until just combined. Gently fold in 1½ cups (210 g) of the blueberries, the lemon zest, and ¼ cup (55 g) of melted butter. Try not to stir the batter again after this.

Heat the æbleskiver pan over low to medium heat with about ½ teaspoon of butter in each cavity. Using an ice cream scoop or a spoon, fill each cavity almost to the top.

Cook until a crust forms on the batter. Using a thin wooden skewer, turn the æbleskiver 90°, letting the batter spill over. Once a skin has formed, the æbleskiver will turn easily. Turn again in a different direction and then a last time to close up the sphere. Spin the æbleskiver around until evenly golden brown and cooked all the way through. Serve right away or keep the æbleskiver warm in a 200°F (100°C) oven.

TO SERVE: Top the æbleskiver with the remaining 1½ cups (210 g) of fresh blueberries and a little bit of the syrup. Serve more syrup on the side.

ALMOND ÆBLESKIVER
WITH WARM MIXED BERRY COMPOTE

Makes about 14 large or 28 small (1½ to 1¾-inch/4 to 4.5-cm) æbleskiver | VG

WARM MIXED BERRY COMPOTE

2 cups (240 g) raspberries

1 cup (240 ml) water

½ cup (100 g) sugar

Juice of 1 lemon

3 tablespoons cornstarch

1 cup (120 g) blackberries

1 cup (140 g) blueberries

1 cup (140 g) strawberries, hulled and cut in half

ÆBLESKIVER

1½ cups (135 g) almond flour

1 cup (140 g) all-purpose flour

1 tablespoon baking powder

½ teaspoon salt

3 tablespoons melted butter + more for the pan

1 cup (100 g) sliced almonds

2 large eggs

1½ cups (360 ml) milk

TO MAKE THE COMPOTE: In a medium saucepan, combine 1 cup (120 g) of the raspberries, the water, sugar, and lemon juice. Bring to a boil over medium heat and cook, stirring occasionally, until the syrup is slightly thickened, about 10 minutes. Transfer the raspberries to a bowl using a slotted spoon and set aside.

In a small bowl, combine the cornstarch in a little water and pour the mixture into the hot liquid in the saucepan, whisking vigorously. Return the pan to the heat and continue whisking until the liquid thickens.

Turn the heat to low and gently fold in the blackberries, blueberries, strawberries, and cooked raspberries. Stir gently until all the berries are warm. Keep warm and set aside.

TO MAKE THE ÆBLESKIVER: Mix the almond flour, all-purpose flour, baking powder, and salt in a large bowl. Set aside.

In a small bowl, combine the 3 tablespoons of melted butter and ½ cup (50 g) of the sliced almonds and stir to evenly coat the almonds. Set aside.

In another small bowl, lightly mix the eggs and milk with a fork and pour the mixture over the flour mixture. Stir quickly until just combined.

Gently fold in the buttered almond slices and try not to stir the batter again after this.

Heat the æbleskiver pan over low to medium heat with about ½ teaspoon of butter in each cavity. Using an ice cream scoop or a spoon, fill each cavity almost to the top.

Cook until a crust forms on the batter. Using a thin wooden skewer, turn the æbleskiver 90°, letting the batter spill over. Once a skin has formed, the æbleskiver will turn easily. Turn again in a different direction and then a last time to close up the sphere. Spin the æbleskiver around until evenly golden brown and cooked all the way through.

TO SERVE: Place the æbleskiver close together on a serving platter, top with the compote, and sprinkle with the remaining ½ cup (50 g) of sliced almonds.

OAT, GINGER, AND PISTACHIO ÆBLESKIVER
WITH ELDERFLOWER GLAZE

Makes about 14 æbleskiver | VG

ELDERFLOWER SYRUP

20 elderflower umbels (clusters)

1 large lemon, thinly sliced

4 cups (960 ml) water

2 cups (400 g) granulated sugar

2 tablespoons citric acid

ELDERFLOWER GLAZE

1½ cups (180 g) powdered sugar

¼ cup (60 ml) Elderflower Syrup (can be replaced with store-bought Elderflower Syrup or Elderflower Liqueur)

ÆBLESKIVER

1 cup (140 g) all-purpose flour

1 cup (120 g) oat flour

1 tablespoon baking powder

¼ teaspoon salt

1¾ cups (420 ml) milk

2 large eggs

2 tablespoons melted butter + more for the pan

¼ cup (40 g) diced crystallized ginger

¾ cup (90 g) roughly chopped pistachios

TO MAKE THE ELDERFLOWER SYRUP: Shake the elderflower clusters to remove loose debris and insects. Avoid rinsing them, as they will lose a lot of flavor. Put the clusters in a large bowl and top with the sliced lemons.

In a saucepan over medium heat, bring the water to a boil. Lower the heat to low, add the granulated sugar, and stir until the sugar has dissolved. Stir in the citric acid and remove the pan from the heat. Pour the hot liquid over the elderflower clusters. Refrigerate for 48 hours, stirring every 12 hours.

Strain the syrup through a cheesecloth and pour into bottles. The syrup will keep for about 4 weeks in the refrigerator but can also be frozen. Makes about 4 cups (960 ml).

TO MAKE THE ELDERFLOWER GLAZE: In a bowl, combine the powdered sugar and ¼ cup (60 ml) of elderflower syrup and beat with a hand mixer until smooth and glossy. If the glaze seems too runny, add a bit more powdered sugar until it reaches the desired consistency. Set aside until ready to serve.

TO MAKE THE ÆBLESKIVER: Combine the flour, oat flour, baking powder, and salt in a large bowl. Set aside.

In a medium bowl, lightly stir together the milk, eggs, and 2 tablespoons of melted butter with a fork. Pour the mixture over the dry ingredients and stir quickly until just combined.

Gently stir in the ginger and ¼ cup (30 g) of the pistachios and try not to stir the batter again after this.

Heat the æbleskiver pan over low to medium heat with about ½ teaspoon of butter in each cavity. Using an ice cream scoop or a spoon, fill each cavity almost to the top.

Cook until a crust forms on the batter. Using a thin wooden skewer, turn the æbleskiver 90°, letting the batter spill over. Once a skin has formed, the æbleskiver will turn easily. Turn again in a different direction and then a last time to close up the sphere. Spin the æbleskiver around until evenly golden brown and cooked all the way through.

TO SERVE: Let the æbleskiver cool to room temperature. Spoon the elderflower glaze over each æbleskiver and garnish with the remaining ½ cup (60 g) of pistachios.

WHITE CHOCOLATE HAZELNUT ÆBLESKIVER
WITH SWEET BEET ICE CREAM AND CANDIED BEET CHIPS

Makes about 14 large or 28 small (1½ to 1¾-inch/4 to 4.5-cm) æbleskiver | VG

1¼ cups (175 g) all-purpose flour

1 teaspoon salt

1 tablespoon baking powder

3 tablespoons sugar

10 ounces (280 g) white chocolate, roughly chopped

½ cup (120 ml) milk

½ cup (120 ml) heavy cream

1 egg

¾ cup (90 g) roasted hazelnuts

Butter, for the pan

Sweet Beet Ice Cream (page 64)

Candied Beet Chips (page 64)

In a large bowl, combine the flour, salt, baking powder, and sugar and mix well. Set aside.

In a separate bowl, place 8 ounces (230 g) of the white chocolate. The remaining will be used for decoration. Set aside.

In a small saucepan over low heat, combine the milk and cream and bring to barely a simmer. Do not boil because white chocolate is extra-sensitive to heat and can burn easily. Remove the pan from the heat and let the liquid cool slightly before pouring it over the chocolate in the bowl. Stir until the chocolate has melted and the mixture is smooth. Set aside to cool to room temperature.

Add the egg and ½ cup (60 g) of the hazelnuts to the white chocolate and mix well. Set aside the remaining ¼ cup (30 g) of hazelnuts for decoration. Pour the mixture over the dry ingredients and stir until just incorporated. Try not to stir the batter again after this.

Heat the æbleskiver pan over low to medium heat with about ½ teaspoon of butter in each cavity. Using an ice cream scoop or a spoon, fill each cavity almost to the top.

Cook until a crust forms on the batter. Using a thin wooden skewer, turn the æbleskiver 90°, letting the batter spill over. Once a skin has formed, the æbleskiver will turn easily. Turn again in a different direction and then a last time to close up the sphere. Spin the æbleskiver around until evenly golden brown and cooked all the way through. Serve right away or keep the æbleskiver warm in a 200°F (100°C) oven.

TO SERVE: Serve the æbleskiver with ice cream and beet chips and top with pieces of the reserved white chocolate and roasted hazelnuts.

SWEET BEET ICE CREAM

Makes about 5½ cups (1.2 k) | GF | VG

1 large beet, peeled
2 cups (480 ml) heavy cream
6 egg yolks
1 cup (240 ml) whole milk
¾ cup (150 g) sugar
Pinch of salt
6 ounces (170 g) white chocolate
1 tablespoon rum or vodka
Zest of 1 orange
Zest of 1 lemon
¼ cup (60 ml) fresh lemon juice

Shred the beet using the fine side of a box grater and add to a large bowl. Add the heavy cream, mix to combine, cover, and refrigerate for 1 to 2 hours.

Strain and squeeze out as much of the liquid as possible. Discard the beet. In the bowl of a stand mixer, whisk the cream to stiff peaks. Refrigerate until ready to use.

In a stainless steel bowl, whisk the egg yolks until light and airy. Set a saucepan of water over low heat and bring to a simmer.

In a separate saucepan over low heat, combine the milk, sugar, and salt, bring to a simmer, and stir for a few minutes until the sugar dissolves. Remove the pot from the heat.

While whisking constantly, slowly pour the hot liquid into the yolks and then place the bowl over the simmering water. Continue to whisk until the mixture thickens enough to coat the back of a spoon, 10 to 15 minutes.

Remove the bowl from the heat. Stir in the white chocolate, rum, orange zest, lemon zest, and lemon juice and keep stirring until the chocolate has melted. Cover and refrigerate until cool.

Gently fold one-third of the custard into the whipped cream. Repeat until all the custard is mixed with the whipped cream. Pour the mixture into a 9-by-5-inch (23-by-12-cm) loaf pan, cover, and freeze for at least 4 hours or overnight.

CANDIED BEET CHIPS

Makes about 2 to 3 cups (325 to 375 g) | GF | V

2 cups (480 ml) water
1 cup (200 g) sugar
3 beets, any color, or a mix, scrubbed and very thinly sliced

Preheat the oven to 200°F (100°C). Line a baking sheet with parchment paper.

In a saucepan over medium heat, bring the water and sugar to a boil. Cook, stirring constantly, until the sugar dissolves. Decrease the heat to low and add the sliced beets. Simmer, stirring occasionally, until the beets are somewhat translucent, about 30 minutes.

Using kitchen tongs, arrange the beet slices in a single layer on the prepared baking sheet, shaking off as much syrup as possible. Bake for 30 minutes. Turn the beet slices. If the parchment is still wet from the syrup, replace with a fresh sheet before turning. Bake for another 30 minutes, until the beet chips are light and crispy. You may need to turn the chips and continue baking to reach the appropriate texture.

CINNAMON RICE ÆBLESKIVER
WITH RISALAMALTA AND STRAWBERRY SYRUP

Makes about 21 æbleskiver | NF | VG

STRAWBERRY SYRUP

4 cups (560 g) sliced fresh strawberries

1½ cups (300 g) granulated sugar

2 cups (480 ml) water

1 tablespoon fresh lemon juice

1 tablespoon cornstarch

ÆBLESKIVER

1 cups (150 g) pearl or sushi rice

2 cups (480 ml) water

1½ teaspoons salt

3 cups (710 ml) whole milk

½ cup (100 g) granulated sugar

1 cinnamon stick

1 cup (240 ml) heavy whipping cream

¼ cup (30 g) powdered sugar

4 large eggs

1 cup (140 g) all-purpose flour

2 teaspoons baking powder

1 tablespoon ground cinnamon

Butter, for the pan

TO MAKE THE STRAWBERRY SYRUP: Set aside half the strawberries.

In a medium saucepan, combine the remaining strawberries, granulated sugar, water, lemon juice, and cornstarch and bring to a boil over medium heat. Lower the heat and simmer until the syrup thickens, 5 to 10 minutes.

Stir in the reserved strawberries and cook over very low heat to keep the berries and syrup warm until ready to serve.

TO MAKE THE ÆBLESKIVER: In a large saucepan, bring the rice, water, and 1 teaspoon of the salt to a boil over medium-high heat. Cover, decrease the heat to low, and simmer for 10 minutes.

Stir in the milk, ¼ cup (50 g) of the granulated sugar, and the cinnamon stick and bring back to a boil. Cover and simmer over low heat until the milk is absorbed, 40 to 45 minutes. Remove the cinnamon stick.

Let cool, then refrigerate to chill completely. Set aside 2 cups (440 g) for the risalamalta and use the remainder, about 4 cups (880 g), for the æbleskiver.

TO MAKE THE RISALAMALTA: In a medium bowl, whip the heavy cream and powdered sugar until stiff peaks form, 3 to 4 minutes. Gently fold the whipped cream into the 2 cups (440 g) of cold rice pudding and return to the refrigerator until ready to serve.

TO FINISH THE ÆBLESKIVER: Stir the eggs into the remaining 4 cups (880 g) of rice pudding until evenly blended. Add the flour, baking powder, ground cinnamon, and remaining ½ teaspoon of salt. Stir until combined.

Heat the æbleskiver pan over low to medium heat with about ½ teaspoon of butter in each cavity. Using an ice cream scoop or a spoon, fill each cavity almost to the top.

Cook until a crust forms on the batter. Using a thin wooden skewer, turn the æbleskiver 90°, letting the batter spill over. Once a skin has formed, the æbleskiver will turn easily. Turn again in a different direction and then a last time to close up the sphere. Spin the æbleskiver around until evenly golden brown and cooked all the way through. Serve right away or keep the æbleskiver warm in a 200°F (100°C) oven.

TO SERVE: Serve the æbleskiver warm with a side of cold risalamalta and topped with warm strawberry syrup.

BLUE CORN ÆBLESKIVER SKEWERS
WITH CITRUS AND BERRY BUTTERCREAM

Makes about 14 æbleskiver or 28 small (1½ to 1¾-inch/4 to 4.5-cm) | NF | VG

BUTTERCREAM FROSTING

- 1 cup (220 g) butter, at room temperature
- 4 cups (480 g) powdered sugar
- Pinch of salt
- 3 to 4 tablespoons cold milk or cream

CITRUS FLAVOR

- 2 tablespoons fresh lemon, lime, or orange juice
- 1 tablespoon lemon, lime, or orange zest

BERRY FLAVOR

- ½ cup (75 g) fresh berries of your choice
- 1 teaspoon fresh lemon juice
- 1 tablespoon granulated sugar

ÆBLESKIVER

- ½ cup (70 g) blue cornmeal
- ¾ cup (105 g) all-purpose flour
- ¼ cup (50 g) granulated sugar
- 3 tablespoons baking powder
- ¼ teaspoon salt
- 1 cup (240 ml) milk
- 1 large egg
- 2 tablespoons melted butter + more for the pan

- Ten 8- to 10-inch (20- to 25-cm) wood or bamboo skewers
- 1 cup (150 g) mixed fresh berries, for garnish
- ¼ lemon, lime, or orange, thinly sliced, for garnish

TO MAKE THE BUTTERCREAM: In a large bowl, use an electric mixer to cream the butter until fluffy. Slowly add in the powdered sugar and salt and continue mixing until well blended.

At this point, divide the mixture in half into individual bowls. One bowl will be for citrus buttercream, and the other will be for berry buttercream.

To make the citrus buttercream, add the fresh juice and zest to one of the bowls and beat with the electric mixer until well combined. If the buttercream is too thick, slowly drizzle in the milk, 1 tablespoon at a time, until it reaches the desired consistency. Beat at high speed until the buttercream is smooth and fluffy.

To make the berry buttercream, combine the berries, lemon juice, and granulated sugar in a small saucepan. Using an immersion blender, puree the mixture. Cook over medium-high heat, stirring often, until half the liquid evaporates. Let cool and then refrigerate until the mixture is completely chilled. Add the chilled berry mixture to the basic buttercream and beat with the electric mixer. If the buttercream is too thick, slowly drizzle in the milk, 1 tablespoon at a time, until it reaches the desired consistency. Beat at high speed until the buttercream is smooth and fluffy.

TO MAKE THE ÆBLESKIVER: Add the cornmeal, flour, granulated sugar, baking powder, and salt to a large bowl and mix well. Set aside.

In a small bowl, lightly mix together the milk, egg, and 2 tablespoons of melted butter with a fork. Pour the mixture over the dry ingredients and stir quickly until just combined. Try not to stir the batter again after this.

Heat the æbleskiver pan over low to medium heat with about ½ teaspoon of butter in each cavity. Using an ice cream scoop or a spoon, fill each cavity almost to the top.

Cook until a crust forms on the batter. Using a thin wooden skewer, turn the æbleskiver 90°, letting the batter spill over. Once a skin has formed, the æbleskiver will turn easily. Turn again in a different direction and then a last time to close up the sphere. Spin the æbleskiver around until evenly golden brown and cooked all the way through. Let cool to room temperature.

TO SERVE: Thread 3 or 4 æbleskiver onto each skewer and set them on a flat surface. Spread with the buttercreams and garnish with the fresh berries and

CHERRY-STUFFED ÆBLESKIVER
WITH HOMEMADE ALMOND PASTE

Makes about 14 æbleskiver | VG

HOMEMADE ALMOND PASTE

1¼ cups (115 g) almond flour

¾ cup (90 g) powdered sugar

¼ cup (60 ml) maple syrup or honey

½ teaspoon almond extract

ÆBLESKIVER

1 recipe Homemade Almond Paste (above)

7 fresh cherries, halved and pitted + more for serving

2 large eggs, separated

1¼ cups (175 g) all-purpose flour

3 tablespoons granulated sugar

1 tablespoon baking powder

½ teaspoon salt

1 cup (240 ml) milk

2 tablespoons melted butter + more for the pan

TO MAKE THE ALMOND PASTE: Combine the almond flour, powdered sugar, maple syrup, and almond extract in a food processor and process until it forms a ball. This will happen in less than a minute.

Shape the paste into a log and wrap in plastic wrap. If the paste is sticky, use a little bit of powdered sugar on your fingertips while working with it. Refrigerate until ready to use.

TO MAKE THE ÆBLESKIVER: Divide the almond paste into 14 equal pieces. Wrap 1 piece of almond paste around 1 half cherry to cover completely. Repeat with the rest of the almond paste and cherries. Set aside.

In a stand mixer, whisk the egg whites until stiff peaks form. Set aside.

In a medium bowl, combine the flour, granulated sugar, baking powder, and salt and mix well. Set aside.

In another bowl, lightly stir together the milk, egg yolks, and 2 tablespoons of melted butter with a fork. Pour the mixture over the dry ingredients and whisk quickly until just combined.

Gently fold the egg whites into the batter until just blended and try not to stir the batter again after this.

Heat the æbleskiver pan over low to medium heat with ½ to 1 teaspoon of butter in each cavity. Once the butter starts to bubble, use an ice cream scoop or a spoon to drop a dollop of batter into each cavity. Put a marzipan-covered cherry on top and push it lightly into the batter. Cover each cavity with more batter.

Cook until a crust forms on the batter. Using a thin wooden skewer to turn the æbleskiver 90°, letting the batter spill over. Turn again in a different direction and then a last time to close up the sphere. Spin the æbleskiver around until evenly golden brown and a toothpick inserted into it comes out mostly clean. Serve right away or keep the æbleskiver warm in a 200°F (100°C) oven.

TO SERVE: Serve the æbleskiver warm with fresh cherries.

GINGERBREAD ÆBLESKIVER
WITH LINGONBERRY CREAM AND HONEY GLAZE

Makes about 21 æbleskiver | GF | VG

GINGERBREAD SPICE

3 tablespoons ground cinnamon

2 tablespoons ground cardamom

2 tablespoons ground ginger

1 teaspoon ground cloves

1 teaspoon ground nutmeg

1 teaspoon ground allspice

1 teaspoon ground white pepper

LINGONBERRY WHIPPED CREAM

6 ounces (170 g) lingonberries + more for garnish

¼ cup (50 g) granulated sugar

1½ cups (360 g) heavy whipping cream

¼ cup (30 g) powdered sugar

HONEY GLAZE

1 cup (120 g) powdered sugar

2 tablespoons honey

1 to 2 teaspoons milk or cream

ÆBLESKIVER

2 cups (200 g) hazelnut flour

½ cup (70 g) sweet rice flour

½ cup (90 g) potato starch

1 cup (200 g) granulated sugar

3 tablespoons Gingerbread Spice (above)

1 teaspoon guar gum

1 tablespoon baking powder

½ teaspoon salt

1 cup (240 ml) milk

3 large eggs

¼ cup (55 g) melted butter + more for the pan

¼ cup (35 g) chopped roasted hazelnuts, for serving

TO MAKE THE GINGERBREAD SPICE: In a container with a tight-fitting lid, mix together all the ingredients. Makes about ½ cup (60 g).

TO MAKE THE LINGONBERRY WHIPPED CREAM: In a small bowl, combine the lingonberries and granulated sugar and stir occasionally until the sugar has dissolved. Set aside.

In a large bowl, beat the cream and powdered sugar with an electric mixer until stiff peaks form. Gently fold in the lingonberry mixture until well blended. Cover and refrigerate until ready to use.

TO MAKE THE HONEY GLAZE: In a medium bowl, combine the powdered sugar and honey. Whisk until well blended and fluffy. The glaze should be thick and glossy with a slow drip. If it's too thick, whisk in milk, 1 teaspoon at a time, until the desired consistency is reached.

TO MAKE THE ÆBLESKIVER: Mix together the hazelnut flour, sweet rice flour, potato starch, granulated sugar, 3 tablespoons of gingerbread spice, guar gum, baking powder, and salt in a large bowl. Set aside.

In a medium bowl, lightly mix together the milk, eggs, and ¼ cup (55 g) of melted butter with a fork. Pour the mixture over the dry ingredients and stir quickly until just combined. Try not to stir the batter again after this.

Heat the æbleskiver pan over low to medium heat with about ½ teaspoon of butter in each cavity. Using an ice cream scoop or a spoon, fill each cavity almost to the top.

Cook until a crust forms on the batter. Using a thin wooden skewer, turn the æbleskiver 90°, letting the batter spill over. Once a skin has formed, the æbleskiver will turn easily. Turn again in a different direction and then a last time to close up the sphere. Spin the æbleskiver around until evenly golden brown and a toothpick inserted into it comes out mostly clean. Serve right away or keep the æbleskiver warm in a 200°F (100°C) oven.

TO SERVE: Cut the tops off the æbleskiver and fill each one with a generous dollop of lingonberry whipped cream. Put the tops back on and drizzle with the honey glaze. Finish by decorating with lingonberries and chopped roasted hazelnuts.

RHUBARB CRUMBLE ÆBLESKIVER
WITH CANDIED RHUBARB AND ICE CREAM

Makes about 14 æbleskiver | VG

RHUBARB JAM

2 pounds (910 g) rhubarb, thinly sliced

2 cups (400 g) granulated sugar

2 tablespoons fresh lemon juice

RHUBARB VANILLA ICE CREAM

2 cups (480 ml) heavy cream

6 egg yolks

1 cup (200 g) granulated sugar

2 tablespoons cornstarch

Pinch of salt

1 cup (240 ml) whole milk

¼ teaspoon pure vanilla powder or seeds from 1 vanilla bean

1 tablespoon rum or vodka

½ cup (160 g) Rhubarb Jam

CANDIED RHUBARB

½ cup (120 ml) water

¾ cup (150 g) granulated sugar

1 tablespoon glucose syrup

2 rhubarb stalks

CONTINUED

TO MAKE THE JAM: In a saucepan over medium-high heat, combine the rhubarb, granulated sugar, and lemon juice and cook, stirring often, until the rhubarb starts to release its juices and the mixture comes to a boil. Continue to cook, stirring occasionally, until the jam thickens, about 45 minutes.

Pour the mixture into an airtight container and refrigerate for up to 2 weeks. Makes about 2 cups (640 g).

TO MAKE THE ICE CREAM: In a stand mixer, whisk the heavy cream until it reaches stiff peaks. Cover and refrigerate.

In a bowl, whisk together the egg yolks, granulated sugar, cornstarch, and salt until light and airy.

In a saucepan over low heat, bring the milk and vanilla to a low boil. Remove the pan from the heat.

While whisking constantly, slowly pour the hot liquid over the egg yolks. Pour the mixture back into the pan.

Continue to whisk over low heat until the mixture starts to bubble on the edges and thickens. Keep whisking for a couple of minutes more before removing the pan from the heat. Add the rum and pour the mixture into a smaller bowl. Cover the surface with plastic wrap and refrigerate until cool.

Gently fold one-third of the custard into the whipped cream. Repeat with the remaining custard and whipped cream.

Layer the custard and jam in a 9-by-5-inch (23-by-12-cm) loaf pan and use a knife to create a swirl. Cover and freeze for at least 4 hours or overnight.

TO MAKE THE CANDIED RHUBARB: Preheat the oven to the lowest setting.

Combine the water and granulated sugar in a saucepan and bring to a boil over high heat. Lower the heat and simmer for 15 minutes. Add the glucose syrup, mix well, and remove the pan from the heat.

Use a peeler to cut the rhubarb into thin strips. Add them to the syrup and soak for 20 minutes.

Spread the rhubarb strips in a single layer on a baking sheet and place in the oven until dry and crisp. Start checking after 15 minutes.

CONTINUED

RHUBARB CRUMBLE ÆBLESKIVER
CONTINUED

CRUMBLE

¼ cup (35 g) all-purpose flour

¼ cup (25 g) rolled oats

¼ cup (50 g) brown sugar

¼ cup (55 g) butter, at room temperature

ÆBLESKIVER

2 cups (280 g) all-purpose flour

¼ cup (50 g) granulated sugar

1 tablespoon baking powder

½ teaspoon salt

2 large eggs

2 cups (480 ml) buttermilk

2 tablespoons melted butter + more for the pan

½ cup (160 g) Rhubarb Jam (page 75)

¼ cup (25 g) sliced almonds

TO MAKE THE CRUMBLE: In a bowl, combine the flour, oats, brown sugar, and butter and mix well. Set aside.

TO MAKE THE ÆBLESKIVER: In a large bowl, combine the flour, granulated sugar, baking powder, and salt. Set aside.

In another bowl, stir together the eggs, buttermilk, and 2 tablespoons of melted butter. Pour the mixture over the dry ingredients and stir quickly until just combined. Try not to stir the batter again after this.

Heat the æbleskiver pan over low to medium heat with ½ to 1 teaspoon of butter in each cavity. Once the butter starts to bubble, use an ice cream scoop or a spoon to drop a dollop of batter into each cavity. Spoon 1 to 1½ teaspoons of rhubarb jam on top. Cover each cavity with more batter. Don't worry if a bit of filling leaks out.

Cook until a crust forms on the batter. Using a thin wooden skewer to turn the æbleskiver 90°, letting the batter spill over. Turn again in a different direction and then a last time to close up the sphere. Spin the æbleskiver around until evenly golden brown and a toothpick inserted into it comes out mostly clean.

Preheat the oven to 225°F (110°C). Grease one large or two smaller baking dishes with butter.

Place the æbleskiver in the prepared baking dish. Spread 1 cup (320 g) of rhubarb jam over the æbleskiver. Roughly cover the top with the crumble and scatter with the sliced almonds. Bake for 20 minutes, or until golden brown.

TO SERVE: Serve the æbleskiver warm with candied rhubarb and rhubarb ice cream.

RED CURRANT HIBISCUS ÆBLESKIVER
WITH CARAMEL JAM AND ZABAGLIONE

Makes about 14 æbleskiver | NF | VG

ZABAGLIONE

1 cup (240 ml) heavy whipping cream

4 egg yolks

¼ cup (50 g) sugar

RED CURRANT CARAMEL JAM WITH A HINT OF HIBISCUS

2 hibiscus tea bags

⅓ cup (80 ml) boiling water

2 cups (250 g) stemmed fresh red currants + more for garnish

2 cups (400 g) sugar

1 cup (240 ml) heavy whipping cream

1 cup (240 ml) light corn syrup

Pinch of salt

CONTINUED

TO MAKE THE ZABAGLIONE: Prepare an ice bath.

In a bowl, beat the heavy whipping cream to firm peaks. Cover and refrigerate.

In another bowl, whisk the yolks and sugar with an electric mixer on high speed until the sugar dissolves and the mixture becomes thick and pale yellow.

Place the bowl over a pan of simmering water and continue to whisk on medium speed until the mixture holds a ribbon.

Take the bowl off the heat and place it in the ice bath. Whisk until cool. Fold in the whipped cream. Refrigerate until ready to use.

TO MAKE THE CARAMEL JAM: Steep the hibiscus tea in the boiling water for 5 to 10 minutes. Remove the tea bags and discard.

Pour the hibiscus tea into a saucepan, add the fresh currants, and bring to a boil over medium-low heat. Boil for about 10 minutes. Remove any foam if needed. Add 1 cup (200 g) of the sugar and boil until the jam thickens, another 15 minutes. Set aside.

In a separate saucepan over medium-high heat, combine the heavy whipping cream, corn syrup, salt, and remaining 1 cup (200 g) of sugar. Bring to a boil and cook, stirring constantly, until the temperature reaches 250°F (120°C) on a candy thermometer (or when the caramel forms a soft ball when dropped into cold water).

Take the caramel off the heat and carefully fold in the red currant mixture. Let cool.

CONTINUED

RED CURRENT HIBISCUS ÆBLESKIVER
CONTINUED

RED CURRANT HIBISCUS ÆBLESKIVER

1¼ cups (175 g) all-purpose flour

1 tablespoon baking powder

½ teaspoon salt

1 cup (240 ml) milk

2 large eggs

2 tablespoons butter + more for the pan

½ cup (160 g) Red Currant Caramel Jam with a Hint of Hibiscus (above)

Edible fresh hibiscus flowers, for garnish (optional)

TO MAKE THE ÆBLESKIVER: Mix the flour, baking powder, and salt in a large bowl. Set aside.

In a small bowl, lightly stir together the milk, eggs, and 2 tablespoons of melted butter with a fork. Pour the mixture over the dry ingredients and whisk quickly until just combined. Try not to stir the batter again after this.

Heat the æbleskiver pan over low to medium heat with ½ to 1 teaspoon of butter in each cavity. Once the butter starts to bubble, use an ice cream scoop or a spoon to drop a dollop of batter into each cavity. Spoon 1 to 1½ teaspoons of caramel jam on top. Cover each cavity with more batter. Don't worry if a bit of filling leaks out.

Cook until a crust forms on the batter. Using a thin wooden skewer to turn the æbleskiver 90°, letting the batter spill over. Turn again in a different direction and then a last time to close up the sphere. Spin the æbleskiver around until evenly golden brown and a toothpick inserted into it comes out mostly clean. Serve right away or keep the æbleskiver warm in a 200°F (100°C) oven.

TO SERVE: Serve the æbleskiver lukewarm with the cold zabaglione and extra jam on the side. Garnish with fresh red currants and edible hibiscus flowers, if using.

BLUEBERRY WHOLE-WHEAT ÆBLESKIVER
WITH BLUEBERRY JAM AND WHIPPED LAVENDER CREAM

Makes about 14 æbleskiver | NF | VG

BLUEBERRY JAM

3 cups (420 g) fresh blueberries

¾ cup (150 g) sugar

¼ cup (60 ml) fresh orange juice

¼ cup (60 ml) Cointreau (can be replaced with orange juice)

WHIPPED LAVENDER CREAM

2 tablespoons honey

2 cups (480 ml) heavy whipping cream

2 tablespoons lavender flowers

ÆBLESKIVER

1 cup (140 g) whole-wheat flour

½ cup (70 g) all-purpose flour

1 tablespoon baking powder

½ teaspoon salt

2 tablespoons melted butter + more for the pan

¼ cup (85 g) honey

2 cups (480 ml) buttermilk

2 large eggs

1 cup (140 g) fresh blueberries + more for garnish

8 to 10 fresh lavender stems, for garnish (optional)

TO MAKE THE BLUEBERRY JAM: In a large pot over medium heat, combine the blueberries, sugar, and orange juice. Bring to a boil and cook, stirring often, until the sugar melts and the berries are starting to burst. Continue to boil until the jam thickens significantly, 25 to 30 minutes. If foam appear on the surface, skim it off with a spoon or spatula.

Remove the pan from the heat and stir in the Cointreau (or orange juice). Pour into jars and refrigerate for up to 2 weeks. Makes about 2 cups (500 g).

TO MAKE THE LAVENDER WHIPPED CREAM: In a small saucepan over medium-low heat, stir together the honey with a little bit of the cream until combined. Add the rest of the cream and the lavender flowers and bring almost to a boil. Remove the pan immediately from the heat.

Strain out the lavender flowers and refrigerate until completely chilled. For a stronger lavender flavor, leave the flowers in and strain just before mixing.

Using an electric mixer, whisk the mixture until stiff peaks form. Refrigerate until ready to serve.

TO MAKE THE ÆBLESKIVER: In a large bowl, combine the whole-wheat flour, all-purpose flour, baking powder, and salt and mix well. Set aside.

In a medium bowl, stir together the 2 tablespoons of melted butter and honey until blended. Add the buttermilk and eggs and stir lightly with a fork. Pour the mixture over the dry ingredients and stir quickly until just combined. Gently stir in the blueberries and try not to stir the batter again after this.

Heat the æbleskiver pan over low to medium heat with about ½ teaspoon of butter in each cavity. Using an ice cream scoop or a spoon, fill each cavity almost to the top.

Cook until a crust forms on the batter. Using a thin wooden skewer, turn the æbleskiver 90°, letting the batter spill over. Once a skin has formed, the æbleskiver will turn easily. Turn again in a different direction and then a last time to close up the sphere. Spin the æbleskiver around until evenly golden brown and a toothpick inserted into it comes out mostly clean. Serve right away or keep the æbleskiver warm in a 200°F (100°C) oven.

TO SERVE: Serve the æbleskiver lukewarm with the blueberry jam and cold whipped lavender cream. Decorate with fresh blueberries strung onto lavender stems (if using).

SWEET SAFFRON ÆBLESKIVER
WITH BLUEBERRY–BLACK CURRANT JAM

Makes about 14 æbleskiver| VG

BLUEBERRY–BLACK CURRANT JAM WITH ALMONDS

3 cups (420 g) fresh blueberries

1½ cups (185 g) fresh black currants

Juice from ½ orange

1 cup (200 g) granulated sugar or (240 ml) maple syrup

½ cup (60 g) roughly chopped blanched almonds

ÆBLESKIVER

1½ cups (210 g) all-purpose flour

1 tablespoon baking powder

½ cup (60 g) powdered sugar

½ teaspoon salt

1 cup (120 g) roughly chopped blanched almonds + more for garnish

2 cups (480 ml) milk

2 large eggs

2 tablespoons melted butter + more for the pan

½ teaspoon ground saffron or 2 teaspoons saffron threads

TO MAKE THE JAM: In a saucepan over medium-high heat, combine the blueberries, currants, orange juice, and granulated sugar and bring to a boil. Cook, stirring occasionally, until the mixture thickens, 15 to 20 minutes.

Remove the pan from the heat and stir in the almonds. Pour into jars and refrigerate for up to 2 weeks. Makes about 2 cups (540 g).

TO MAKE THE ÆBLESKIVER: Combine the flour, baking powder, powdered sugar, and salt in a large bowl and mix well. Stir in the almonds and set aside.

In another bowl, lightly mix together the milk, eggs, 2 tablespoons of melted butter, and saffron. Pour the mixture over the dry ingredients and stir quickly until just combined. Try not to stir the batter again after this.

Heat the æbleskiver pan over low to medium heat with about ½ teaspoon of butter in each cavity. Using an ice cream scoop or a spoon, fill each cavity almost to the top.

Cook until a crust forms on the batter. Using a thin wooden skewer, turn the æbleskiver 90°, letting the batter spill over. Once a skin has formed, the æbleskiver will turn easily. Turn again in a different direction and then a last time to close up the sphere. Spin the æbleskiver around until evenly golden brown and a toothpick inserted into it comes out mostly clean. Serve right away or keep the æbleskiver warm in a 200°F (100°C) oven.

TO SERVE: Serve the æbleskiver warm with the jam and garnish with chopped almonds.

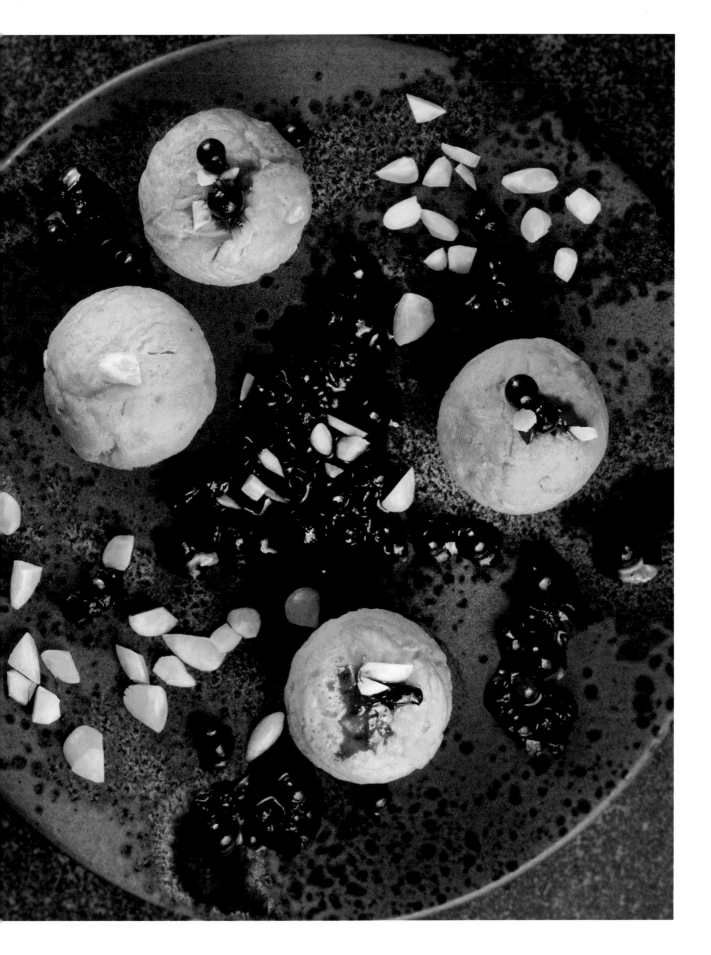

CHOCOLATE TRUFFLE ÆBLESKIVER
WITH CHOCOLATE GLAZE

Makes about 14 æbleskiver | NF | VG

CHOCOLATE GANACHE TRUFFLE FILLING

8 ounces (230 g) chocolate, chips or chopped

½ cup (120 ml) heavy cream

CHOCOLATE GLAZE

1½ cups (180 g) powdered sugar

¼ cup (20 g) cocoa powder

1 to 3 tablespoons water

ÆBLESKIVER

1½ cups (210 g) all-purpose flour

1 tablespoon baking powder

2 tablespoons granulated sugar

¼ teaspoon salt

1¼ cups (300 ml) milk

1 egg

3 tablespoons melted butter + more for the pan

½ cup (120 g) Chocolate Ganache Truffle Filling (above)

Fresh or dried edible flowers, for garnish (optional)

TO MAKE THE GANACHE: Place the chocolate in a heatproof bowl. In a saucepan over medium-low heat, bring the heavy cream to a simmer, stirring occasionally. Remove from the heat, pour the hot cream over the chocolate, and let sit for a few minutes. Stir the mixture until smooth. Refrigerate.

TO MAKE THE GLAZE: In a medium bowl, stir together the powdered sugar and cocoa powder. Slowly add the water, 1 tablespoon at a time, and stir until evenly mixed, adding as much water as needed until it reaches a thick but pourable consistency. Set aside.

TO MAKE THE ÆBLESKIVER: In a large bowl, add the flour, baking powder, granulated sugar, and salt and mix well. Set aside.

In another bowl, lightly mix together the milk, egg, and 3 tablespoons of melted butter with a fork. Pour the mixture over the dry ingredients and stir quickly until just combined. Try not to stir the batter again after this.

Heat the æbleskiver pan over low to medium heat with ½ to 1 teaspoon of butter in each cavity. Once the butter starts to bubble, use an ice cream scoop or a spoon to drop a dollop of batter into each cavity. Spoon 1 to 1½ teaspoons of chocolate ganache on top and push it down lightly. Cover each cavity with more batter. Don't worry if a bit of filling leaks out.

Cook until a crust forms on the batter. Using a thin wooden skewer to turn the æbleskiver 90°, letting the batter spill over. Turn again in a different direction and then a last time to close up the sphere. Spin the æbleskiver around until evenly golden brown and a toothpick inserted into it comes out mostly clean. Let the æbleskiver cool to room temperature.

TO SERVE: Place the æbleskiver on a serving platter and pour the slightly cooled chocolate glaze over the tops. Garnish with edible flowers (if using). These can be placed on a table or passed around and eaten out of hand.

BUTTERSCOTCH MIDSUMMER WREATH
WITH WHIPPED CREAM AND FRESH BERRIES

Serves 6 to 8 | NF | VG

BUTTERSCOTCH
¾ cup (165 g) butter
1½ cups (300 g) brown sugar
¾ cup (180 ml) heavy cream
pinch of salt

WHIPPED CREAM
1 cup (240 ml) heavy whipping cream
1 tablespoon powdered sugar

BUTTERSCOTCH ÆBLESKIVER
1 cup (140 g) all-purpose flour
1 cup (160 g) fine semolina flour
1 tablespoon baking powder
½ teaspoon salt
¼ cup (50 g) granulated sugar
3 large eggs
1½ cups (360 ml) milk
½ cup (120 g) sour cream
2 tablespoons melted butter + more for the pan
½ cup (120 ml) Butterscotch (above) or store-bought

2 cups (300 g) mixed berries
Edible flowers such as strawberry, chamomile, and cornflowers, for garnish (optional)

TO MAKE THE BUTTERSCOTCH: Combine the butter, brown sugar, heavy cream, and salt in a medium pan over medium heat. Bring to a boil and let boil for 10 minutes. Remove from the heat and set aside to cool to room temperature. Makes about 1½ cups (600 g).

TO MAKE THE WHIPPED CREAM: In a medium bowl, whip the cream and powdered sugar with an electric mixer until medium to stiff peaks form. Transfer the mixture to a piping bag and refrigerate until ready to use.

TO MAKE THE ÆBLESKIVER: Combine the flour, semolina, baking powder, salt, and granulated sugar in a large bowl and mix well. Set aside.

In another bowl, lightly stir together the eggs, milk, sour cream, and 2 tablespoons of melted butter with a fork. Pour the mixture over the dry ingredients and stir quickly until just combined. Gently fold in the ½ cup (120 ml) of butterscotch and try not to stir the batter again after this.

Heat the æbleskiver pan over low to medium heat with about ½ teaspoon of butter in each cavity. Using an ice cream scoop or a spoon, fill each cavity almost to the top.

Cook until a crust forms on the batter. Using a thin wooden skewer, turn the æbleskiver 90°, letting the batter spill over. Once a skin has formed, the æbleskiver will turn easily. Turn again in a different direction and then a last time to close up the sphere. Spin the æbleskiver around until evenly golden brown and a toothpick inserted into it comes out mostly clean.

Place the æbleskiver in a circle on the outer edge of a plate. Add another circle inside and a third circle balancing on top in between the first two rings. Using a piping bag with a small tip, pipe the butterscotch randomly on and around the wreath.

TO SERVE: Place the mixed berries all over and around the æbleskiver wreath. Decorate with edible flowers (if using). Serve the remaining berries on the side along with the whipped cream.

COFFEE CRUMBLE ÆBLESKIVER
WITH WALNUTS AND SWEET ESPRESSO DIP

Makes about 21 æbleskiver | VG

SWEET ESPRESSO DIP

4 cups (480 g) powdered sugar

6 tablespoons milk or cream

1 to 2 tablespoons espresso powder

COFFEE CRUMBLE

3 tablespoons butter

½ cup (100 g) brown sugar

¼ cup (50 g) granulated sugar

1 cup (120 g) chopped walnuts

2 teaspoons instant espresso powder

½ teaspoon salt

ÆBLESKIVER

1½ cups (210 g) all-purpose flour

1½ cups (150 g) rolled oats

½ cup (100 g) brown sugar

1 tablespoon baking powder

½ teaspoon salt

1 teaspoon espresso powder

2 large eggs

2 cups (480 ml) milk

1 cup (120 g) chopped walnuts

¼ cup (55 g) melted butter + more for the pan

2 tablespoons coffee beans, for garnish (optional)

TO MAKE THE ESPRESSO DIP: In a large bowl, combine the powdered sugar, milk, and 1 tablespoon of the espresso powder and beat with an electric mixer until well blended. Taste and add up to 1 tablespoon more espresso powder to reach your desired coffee flavor. Set aside.

TO MAKE THE COFFEE CRUMBLE: Melt the butter in a small pan over medium-low heat. Add the brown sugar, granulated sugar, walnuts, espresso powder, and salt and stir over low heat until the sugar gets a bit gooey and starts sticking to the walnuts. It will take only a few minutes. Spread the nut mixture onto a baking sheet and set aside until cooled.

TO MAKE THE ÆBLESKIVER: In a large bowl, combine the flour, oats, brown sugar, baking powder, salt, and espresso powder and mix well. Set aside.

In another bowl, lightly whisk together the eggs, milk, walnuts, and ¼ cup (55 g) of melted butter. Pour the mixture over the dry ingredients and whisk quickly until just combined. Try not to stir the batter again after this.

Heat the æbleskiver pan over low to medium heat with ½ to 1 teaspoon of butter in each cavity. Using an ice cream scoop or a spoon, fill each cavity almost to the top.

Cook until a crust forms on the batter. Using a thin wooden skewer, turn the æbleskiver 90°, letting the batter spill over. Once a skin has formed, the æbleskiver will turn easily. Turn again in a different direction and then a last time to close up the sphere. Spin the æbleskiver around until evenly golden brown and a toothpick inserted into it comes out mostly clean. Serve right away or keep the æbleskiver warm in a 200°F (100°C) oven.

TO SERVE: Serve the æbleskiver with a generous amount of coffee crumble sprinkled over the top and on the plate, with the espresso dip on the side. Garnish with coffee beans (if using).

WILD STRAWBERRY ÆBLESKIVER
WITH STRAWBERRY CURD AND GLAZE

Makes about 21 æbleskiver | NF | VG

STRAWBERRY CURD

1 pound (455 g) fresh strawberries

1 cup (340 g) honey

¼ cup (60 ml) fresh lemon juice

4 large eggs

½ cup (110 g) cold butter, cubed

STRAWBERRY–WHITE CHOCOLATE GLAZE

8 ounces (230 g) white chocolate, roughly chopped

¼ cup (60 ml) heavy whipping cream

¼ cup (60 g) Strawberry Curd

ÆBLESKIVER

1 cup (140 g) all-purpose flour

1¼ cups (200 g) semolina flour

¼ cup (50 g) sugar

1 tablespoon baking powder

½ teaspoon salt

2 large eggs

2 cups (480 ml) milk

2 tablespoons melted butter + more for the pan

½ cup (120 g) Strawberry Curd (above)

Fresh strawberries, for garnish

6 to 8 grass straws, for serving (optional)

TO MAKE THE STRAWBERRY CURD: Mash the strawberries in a bowl or use a food processor and process until pureed.

In a saucepan over medium-high heat, combine the strawberry puree, honey, and lemon juice, bring to a boil, and cook until the liquid is mostly reduced, about 20 minutes. Let the mixture cool until it's lukewarm.

Whisk the eggs into the strawberry mixture. Transfer the mixture to a double boiler over simmering water and cook, constantly scraping the bottom of the pan with a wooden spoon or spatula, until the curd is thick enough to coat the back of a spoon, 5 to 10 minutes. Don't worry if it takes longer.

Remove the pan from the heat, add the cubed butter, and stir until incorporated. Cover and refrigerate until ready to use. Makes about 3 cups (720 g).

TO MAKE THE GLAZE: Place the white chocolate in a heatproof bowl. In a saucepan over medium-low heat, bring the heavy whipping cream to a simmer. Pour the hot cream over the white chocolate and stir gently until the chocolate is melted. Let cool slightly. Fold in the strawberry curd. Set aside.

TO MAKE THE ÆBLESKIVER: In a large bowl, combine the flour, semolina, sugar, baking powder, and salt and mix well. Set aside. In another bowl, stir together the eggs, milk, and 2 tablespoons of melted butter. Pour the mixture over the dry ingredients and stir quickly until just combined. Try not to stir the batter again after this.

Heat the æbleskiver pan over low to medium heat with ½ to 1 teaspoon of butter in each cavity. Once the butter starts to bubble, use an ice cream scoop or a spoon to drop a dollop of batter into each cavity. Spoon 1 teaspoon of strawberry curd on top. Cover each cavity with more batter. Don't worry if a bit of filling leaks out.

Cook until a crust forms on the batter. Using a thin wooden skewer to turn the æbleskiver 90°, letting the batter spill over. Turn again in a different direction and then a last time to close up the sphere. Spin the æbleskiver around until evenly golden brown and a toothpick inserted into it comes out mostly clean. Let them cool slightly.

Dip each æbleskiver in the glaze, twirling and rotating to coat the tops. If you prefer, you can spoon the glaze over the tops instead.

TO SERVE: Arrange a few æbleskiver on each plate and garnish with strawberries threaded onto grass straws (if using) or scattered on the plate. Serve more curd on the side.

CHOCOLATE AND BACON ÆBLESKIVER
WITH SPICY CHOCOLATE GLAZE

Makes about 14 æbleskiver | NF

SPICY CHOCOLATE GLAZE

1 cup (240 ml) whole milk

¼ teaspoon ground cinnamon

⅛ teaspoon cayenne pepper

2 cups (360 g) chocolate, chips or chopped

ÆBLESKIVER

1½ cups (210 g) all-purpose flour

1 tablespoon baking powder

½ teaspoon salt

2 large eggs

2 cups (480 ml) milk or buttermilk

1 cup (180 g) chocolate chips

14 ounces (400 g) crispy cooked bacon, chopped

Butter, for the pan

TO MAKE THE GLAZE: Heat the milk, cinnamon, and cayenne in a saucepan until the mixture begins to steam. Remove the pan from the heat and stir in the chocolate. Continue to stir until all the chocolate has melted completely and the glaze has a smooth consistency. Set aside.

TO MAKE THE ÆBLESKIVER: Combine the flour, baking powder, and salt in a large bowl and set aside.

In a separate bowl, lightly stir together the eggs and milk with a fork. Pour the mixture over the dry ingredients and stir quickly until just combined. Gently stir in the chocolate chips and 10 ounces (280 g) of the cooked bacon and try not to stir the batter again after this.

Heat the æbleskiver pan over low to medium heat with ½ to 1 teaspoon of butter in each cavity. Using an ice cream scoop or a spoon, fill each cavity almost to the top.

Cook until a crust forms on the batter. Using a thin wooden skewer, turn the æbleskiver 90°, letting the batter spill over. Once a skin has formed, the æbleskiver will turn easily. Turn again in a different direction and then a last time to close up the sphere. Spin the æbleskiver around until evenly golden brown and a toothpick inserted into it comes out mostly clean. Serve right away or keep the æbleskiver warm in a 200°F (100°C) oven.

TO SERVE: Place the æbleskiver on a serving platter. Pour the spicy chocolate glaze over the top and garnish with the remaining 4 ounces (120 g) of crispy chopped bacon. These can be placed on a table or be passed around and eaten out of hand like donuts.

CHOCOLATE CARAMEL ÆBLESKIVER
WITH RUM-RAISIN CARAMEL ICE CREAM

Makes about 21 æbleskiver | VG

CHOCOLATE, NUT, AND RAISIN CARAMEL

2 cups (280 g) golden raisins

¾ cup (180 ml) rum

½ cup (120 ml) maple syrup

¼ cup (90 g) honey

½ cup (50 g) sugar

2 tablespoons butter

2 tablespoons heavy cream

1 cup (180 g) chocolate chips

1 cup (120 g) chopped walnuts

1 cup (120 g) chopped pecans

½ teaspoon salt

CHOCOLATE, NUT, AND RAISIN CARAMEL ICE CREAM

2 cups (480 ml) cold heavy cream

One 14-ounce (400-g) can sweetened condensed milk

¼ cup (60 ml) rum

1½ cups (300 g) Chocolate, Nut, and Raisin Caramel (above)

ÆBLESKIVER

1½ cups (210 g) all-purpose flour

1 tablespoon baking powder

½ teaspoon salt

2 large eggs

2 cups (480 ml) buttermilk

1½ cups (300 g) Chocolate, Nut, and Raisin Caramel (above)

Butter, for the pan

TO MAKE THE CARAMEL: Soak the golden raisins in the rum overnight. Strain and save the rum and the soaked raisins separately.

Combine the syrup, honey, sugar, butter, cream, and leftover rum (if using) and bring to a boil over low heat. Simmer until it reaches a syrup consistency that easily coats a spoon, 20 to 30 minutes. Let cool completely.

Stir in the chocolate chips, walnuts, pecans, salt, and soaked raisins. Set aside.

TO MAKE THE ICE CREAM: Beat the cold whipping cream with an electric mixer until it reaches stiff peaks.

In a separate bowl, combine the condensed milk and the strained rum and mix well. Carefully add half of the whipped cream and stir until smooth. Gently fold in the remaining whipped cream and stir until just blended.

In a freezer-safe container, alternate layers of the cream mixture with the caramel, about a third at a time, spreading each layer evenly all the way to the sides, and make a swirl on top. Cover and freeze overnight.

TO MAKE THE ÆBLESKIVER: In a large bowl, mix together the flour, baking powder, and salt. Set aside.

In another bowl, lightly mix together the eggs and buttermilk with a fork. Pour the mixture over the dry ingredients and whisk quickly until just combined. Gently stir in the caramel without completely blending, leaving large chunks of the caramel unmixed. Try not to stir the batter again after this.

Heat the æbleskiver pan over low to medium heat with ½ to 1 teaspoon of butter in each cavity. Using an ice cream scoop or a spoon, fill each cavity almost to the top.

Cook until a crust forms on the batter. Using a thin wooden skewer, turn the æbleskiver 90°, letting the batter spill over. Once a skin has formed, the æbleskiver will turn easily. Turn again in a different direction and then a last time to close up the sphere. Spin the æbleskiver around until evenly golden brown and a toothpick inserted into it comes out mostly clean. Serve right away or keep the æbleskiver warm in a 200°F (100°C) oven.

TO SERVE: Serve the æbleskiver with scoops of ice cream and the remaining caramel mixture, about 1½ cups (300 g).

CRUNCHY CINNAMON ÆBLESKIVER
WITH DARK CHOCOLATE DIPPING SAUCE

Makes about 14 æbleskiver | NF | VG

DARK CHOCOLATE SAUCE

⅔ cup (160 ml) evaporated milk

6 ounces (170 g) dark chocolate

¼ cup (55 g) butter, cubed

½ teaspoon ground cinnamon

⅔ cup (130 g) raw sugar

ÆBLESKIVER

1½ cups (210 g) all-purpose flour

4 teaspoons baking powder

½ teaspoon salt

¼ cup (50 g) raw sugar

1 teaspoon ground cinnamon

1 egg

1¼ cups (300 ml) milk

½ teaspoon vanilla extract

¾ cup (165 g) melted butter + more for the pan

½ cup (100 g) raw sugar

2 tablespoons ground cinnamon

TO MAKE THE DARK CHOCOLATE SAUCE: In a saucepan over medium-low heat, bring the evaporated milk to a simmer. Remove from the heat and add the chocolate, butter, cinnamon, and raw sugar and stir until melted.

Return the pan to medium-low heat and bring the mixture to a low boil. Decrease the heat to low and simmer, stirring constantly, for 5 minutes. Remove from the heat. Let cool slightly before serving.

TO MAKE THE ÆBLESKIVER: In a large bowl, combine the flour, baking powder, salt, raw sugar, and cinnamon and mix well. Set aside.

In another bowl, mix together the egg, milk, vanilla, and ¼ cup (55 g) of the melted butter. Pour the mixture over the dry ingredients and whisk quickly until just combined. Try not to stir the batter again after this.

Heat the æbleskiver pan over low to medium heat with ½ to 1 teaspoon of butter in each cavity. Using an ice cream scoop or a spoon, fill each cavity almost to the top.

Cook until a crust forms on the batter. Using a thin wooden skewer, turn the æbleskiver 90°, letting the batter spill over. Once a skin has formed, the æbleskiver will turn easily. Turn again in a different direction and then a last time to close up the sphere. Spin the æbleskiver around until evenly golden brown and a toothpick inserted into it comes out mostly clean. Serve right away or keep the æbleskiver warm in a 200°F (100°C) oven.

TO SERVE: In a small bowl, mix together the raw sugar and cinnamon. Brush the warm æbleskiver with the remaining ½ cup (110 g) of melted butter and roll each one in the sugar and cinnamon mixture. Serve with the chocolate dipping sauce on the side.

CHOCOLATE COCONUT ÆBLESKIVER
AND CHOCOLATE SAUCE WITH A HINT OF MINT

Makes about 14 large or 28 small (1½ to 1¾-inch/4 to 4.5-cm) æbleskiver | GF | NF | VG

CHOCOLATE SAUCE WITH A HINT OF MINT

½ cup (120 ml) coconut oil

8 ounces (230 g) chocolate, chips or chopped

¼ teaspoon peppermint extract

ÆBLESKIVER

1 cup (140 g) sweet rice flour

½ cup (70 g) brown rice flour

¼ cup (45 g) potato starch

2 tablespoons tapioca starch

1 teaspoon guar gum

¼ cup (50 g) sugar

1 tablespoon baking powder

½ teaspoon salt

2 cups (480 ml) buttermilk

2 large eggs

½ teaspoon vanilla extract

¼ cup (55 g) melted butter + more for the pan

1 cup (180 g) chocolate chips

½ cup (40 g) unsweetened coconut flakes

Fourteen 6- to 8-inch (~o-cm) bamboo skewers

TO MAKE THE CHOCOLATE SAUCE: Warm the coconut oil in a small saucepan over low heat until melted. Remove the pan from the heat, add the chocolate and peppermint extract, and stir until the chocolate is melted and the sauce is smooth. Keep warm until ready to serve.

TO MAKE THE ÆBLESKIVER: In a large bowl, combine the sweet rice flour, brown rice flour, potato starch, tapioca starch, guar gum, sugar, baking powder, and salt and mix well. Set aside.

In another bowl, mix together the buttermilk, eggs, vanilla, and ¼ cup (55 g) of melted butter until combined. Pour the mixture over the dry ingredients and whisk quickly until just combined. Gently fold in the chocolate chips and coconut flakes. Try not to stir the batter again after this.

Heat the æbleskiver pan over low to medium heat with ½ to 1 teaspoon of butter in each cavity. Using an ice cream scoop or a spoon, fill each cavity almost to the top.

Cook until a crust forms on the batter. Using a thin wooden skewer, turn the æbleskiver 90°, letting the batter spill over. Once a skin has formed, the æbleskiver will turn easily. Turn again in a different direction and then a last time to close up the sphere. Spin the æbleskiver around until evenly golden brown and a toothpick inserted into it comes out mostly clean. Serve right away or keep the æbleskiver warm in a 200°F (100°C) oven.

TO SERVE: Put each æbleskiver on individual bamboo skewers and place them on a serving platter. Serve the warm chocolate sauce in a bowl for dipping.

ZEBRA ÆBLESKIVER
WITH CHOCOLATE MARBLE SAUCE

Makes about 21 large or 42 small (1½ to 1¾-inch/4 to 4.5-cm) æbleskiver | NF | VG

CHOCOLATE MARBLE SAUCE

1 cup (180 g) dark chocolate chips

1 cup (180 g) white chocolate chips

1½ cups (360 ml) heavy cream

VANILLA BATTER

1 cup (140 g) all-purpose flour

3 tablespoons sugar

1 teaspoon baking powder

Pinch of salt

½ teaspoon pure vanilla powder

1 cup (240 ml) milk

1 large egg

1 tablespoon vegetable oil

CHOCOLATE BATTER

¾ cup (105 g) all-purpose flour

¼ cup (50 g) sugar

¼ cup (20 g) cocoa powder

1 teaspoon baking powder

Pinch of salt

1 cup (240 ml) milk

1 large egg

1 tablespoon vegetable oil

Butter, for the pan

TO MAKE THE SAUCE: Put the dark and white chocolates in separate heatproof bowls. Heat the heavy cream in a small saucepan over medium heat and remove it just as it starts to steam. Pour half of the warm cream over each of the chocolates and stir until evenly mixed and smooth.

TO MAKE THE VANILLA BATTER: In a medium bowl, add the flour, sugar, baking powder, salt, and vanilla powder and mix well. Set aside.

In another bowl, lightly mix together the milk, egg, and vegetable oil with a fork. Pour the mixture over the dry ingredients and whisk quickly until just combined. Try not to stir the batter again after this.

TO MAKE THE CHOCOLATE BATTER: In a medium bowl, add the flour, sugar, cocoa, baking powder, and salt and mix well. Set aside.

In another bowl, lightly mix together the milk, egg, and vegetable oil with a fork. Pour the mixture over the dry ingredients and whisk quickly until just combined. Try not to stir the batter again after this.

Heat the æbleskiver pan over low to medium heat with ½ to 1 teaspoon of butter in each cavity. For a zebra look, use a dual-color piping bag and pipe the batters into the pan with a spiral movement. Without a dual-color piping bag you can simply alternate spooning in the vanilla and chocolate batters to create cow-patterned æbleskiver. Fill each cavity almost to the top.

Cook until a crust forms on the batter. Using a thin wooden skewer, turn the æbleskiver 90°, letting the batter spill over. Once a skin has formed, the æbleskiver will turn easily. Turn again in a different direction and then a last time to close up the sphere. Spin the æbleskiver around until evenly golden brown and a toothpick inserted into it comes out mostly clean. Serve right away or keep the æbleskiver warm in a 200°F (100°C) oven.

TO SERVE: Pour a few spoonfuls of the dark chocolate sauce onto each serving plate. Pour dollops of the white chocolate sauce randomly over the dark. Using a toothpick, move the white chocolate around to create a swirl pattern. Place the æbleskiver on top.

CHOCOLATE LAVA ÆBLESKIVER
WITH WHIPPED CREAM AND GOLD LEAF

Makes about 14 large or 28 small (1½ to 1¾-inch/4 to 4.5-cm) æbleskiver | NF | VG

WHIPPED CREAM
1 cup (240 ml) heavy cream
¼ cup (30 g) powdered sugar

ÆBLESKIVER
1½ cups (210 g) all-purpose flour
2 teaspoons baking powder
pinch of salt
1 cup (220 g) melted butter + more for the pan
2½ cups (500 g) granulated sugar
½ cup (50 g) cocoa powder
6 eggs

Crushed cocoa beans, for garnish
Edible gold leaf, for garnish

TO MAKE THE WHIPPED CREAM: Using an electric mixer, whisk the heavy cream and powdered sugar until stiff peaks form. Refrigerate until ready to serve.

TO MAKE THE ÆBLESKIVER: A nonstick pan is highly recommended for this recipe.

In a large bowl, add the flour, baking powder, and salt and mix well. Set aside.

Melt the butter in a medium saucepan over low heat. Add the granulated sugar and cocoa powder, and stir until well blended. Remove from the heat and stir in the eggs.

Pour the mixture over the dry ingredients and whisk quickly until just combined. Try not to stir the batter again after this.

Heat the æbleskiver pan over low heat with ½ to 1 teaspoon of butter in each cavity. Using an ice cream scoop or a spoon, fill each cavity almost to the top.

Cook slowly until a crust forms on the batter. Use a small spoon to gently lift up and turn the æbleskiver 90°, letting the batter spill over. These æbleskiver are especially delicate, but be patient; once a skin has formed, the æbleskiver will turn more easily. Use the spoon to tuck any of the overflowing batter back into each well before turning again in a different direction and then a last time to close up the sphere. The æbleskiver are done as soon as a crust is formed all around and the æbleskiver hold together. They should be gooey inside.

Serve right away or let the æbleskiver cool to room temperature.

TO SERVE: Place the æbleskiver on a large serving platter or on individual plates. Use a few different size and style of piping tips to decorate the plate with the whipped cream. Sprinkle with a few crushed cocoa beans and garnish with small, torn pieces of gold leaf.

SAVORY
ÆBLESKIVER

RICOTTA SALATA ÆBLESKIVER
WITH GRILLED CORN AND FRESH HERB SPREAD

Makes about 21 æbleskiver | NF | VG

FRESH HERB SPREAD

1½ cups (185 g) shaved ricotta salata

¼ cup (10 g) finely chopped fresh parsley

2 tablespoons finely chopped fresh mint

2 tablespoons finely chopped fresh chives

2 tablespoons finely chopped fresh dill

1½ cups (360 g) crème fraîche

Juice of ½ lemon

Pepper

GRILLED CORN

6 ears corn, shucked

¼ cup (55 g) melted butter

Salt

ÆBLESKIVER

2 large eggs, separated

2 cups (280 g) all-purpose flour

2 tablespoons sugar

2 teaspoon baking powder

½ teaspoon baking soda

½ teaspoon salt

2 cups (480 ml) milk

2 tablespoons melted butter + more for the pan

½ cup (60 g) shaved ricotta salata + more for serving

2 tablespoons finely chopped fresh parsley

2 tablespoons finely chopped fresh dill

TO MAKE THE HERB SPREAD: Set aside a pinch each of the ricotta salata, parsley, mint, chives, and dill. In a bowl, combine the crème fraîche and the remaining ricotta salata, parsley, mint, chives, dill, and lemon juice and mix well. Sprinkle the reserved cheese and herbs over the top and season with a little pepper. Cover and refrigerate until ready to serve.

TO MAKE THE GRILLED CORN: Preheat a grill until well heated. Grill the corn, turning often, until lightly charred, about 10 minutes.

Brush with the melted butter and season with salt. Using a sharp knife, cut the corn off the cobs until you have 1½ cups (225 g) for the æbleskiver, plus some extra for serving. Cut the rest of the cobs into quarters and keep warm until ready to serve.

TO MAKE THE ÆBLESKIVER: In a stand mixer, whisk the egg whites until they form stiff peaks. Set aside.

In a medium bowl, combine the flour, sugar, baking powder, baking soda, and salt and mix well. Set aside.

In another bowl, stir together the milk, egg yolks, 2 tablespoons of melted butter, reserved corn kernels, ½ cup (60 g) of ricotta salata, the parsley, and dill. Pour the mixture over the dry ingredients and whisk quickly until just combined.

Gently fold the egg whites into the batter and try not to stir the batter again after this.

Heat the æbleskiver pan over low to medium heat with ½ to 1 teaspoon of butter in each cavity. Using an ice cream scoop or a spoon, fill each cavity almost to the top.

Cook until a crust forms on the batter. Using a thin wooden skewer, turn the æbleskiver 90°, letting the batter spill over. Once a skin has formed, the æbleskiver will turn easily. Turn again in a different direction and then a last time to close up the sphere. Spin the æbleskiver around until evenly golden brown and a toothpick inserted into it comes out mostly clean. Serve right away or keep the æbleskiver warm in a 200°F (100°C) oven.

TO SERVE: Serve the æbleskiver with the grilled corn quarters and herb spread.

CHEDDAR AND CHIVE ÆBLESKIVER
WITH AVOCADO AND ENDIVE SALAD AND BUTTERMILK DRESSING

Makes about 14 æbleskiver | NF | VG

BUTTERMILK DRESSING

1 cup (240 ml) buttermilk

½ cup (120 ml) sour cream

½ cup (120 ml) mayonnaise

1 tablespoon fresh lemon juice

¼ cup (15 g) finely chopped chives + more for serving

Salt and pepper

AVOCADO AND ENDIVE SALAD

4 heads endive

2 avocados, pitted, peeled, and sliced

Micro chives and flowers (optional)

ÆBLESKIVER

1½ cups (210 g) all-purpose flour

1 tablespoon baking powder

1 teaspoon sugar

½ teaspoon salt

2 cups (480 ml) buttermilk

2 large eggs

¼ cup (55 g) melted butter + more for the pan

1 cup (80 g) shredded Cheddar cheese

¼ cup (15 g) finely chopped fresh chives

TO MAKE THE DRESSING: In a bowl, mix together the buttermilk, sour cream, mayonnaise, lemon juice, and ¼ cup (15 g) of chives. Season with salt and pepper to taste. Cover and refrigerate until ready to use.

TO MAKE THE SALAD: Cut the endive heads into quarters lengthwise and divide them among four plates, leaving about half the plate empty for the æbleskiver. Top the endive with slices of avocado. Drizzle the dressing over the top. Sprinkle with chopped chives and micro chives and flowers (if using).

TO MAKE THE ÆBLESKIVER: In a large bowl, combine the flour, baking powder, sugar, and salt and mix well. Set aside.

In another bowl, lightly mix together the buttermilk, eggs, ¼ cup (55 g) of melted butter, shredded cheese, and chopped chives with a fork. Pour the mixture over the dry ingredients and whisk quickly until just combined. Try not to stir the batter again after this.

Heat the æbleskiver pan over low to medium heat with ½ to 1 teaspoon of butter in each cavity. Using an ice cream scoop or a spoon, fill each cavity almost to the top.

Cook until a crust forms on the batter. Using a thin wooden skewer, turn the æbleskiver 90°, letting the batter spill over. Once a skin has formed, the æbleskiver will turn easily. Turn again in a different direction and then a last time to close up the sphere. Spin the æbleskiver around until evenly golden brown and a toothpick inserted into it comes out mostly clean. Serve right away or keep the æbleskiver warm in a 200°F (100°C) oven.

TO SERVE: Serve the æbleskiver warm with the salad.

CAULIFLOWER ÆBLESKIVER
WITH PEPPER AND EXTRA CHEESE

Makes about 14 æbleskiver | GF | NF | VG

6 tablespoons butter + more for the pan

2 garlic cloves, chopped

½ teaspoon salt

¼ teaspoon cayenne pepper

Pinch of white pepper

2 cups (200 g) riced cauliflower

1 cup (240 ml) milk

2 large eggs

½ cup (75 g) fine-grind yellow corn flour

¼ cup (40 g) medium-grind yellow cornmeal

2 tablespoons potato starch

1 tablespoon tapioca starch

1 tablespoon baking powder

1 teaspoon guar gum

½ cup (50 g) grated Parmesan cheese

1 cup (80 g) shredded Cheddar cheese

Crushed pink peppercorns, for garnish

Pieces of multicolored cauliflower and micro greens, for garnish (optional)

Melt the 6 tablespoons of butter in a frying pan over medium heat. Add the garlic and sauté until it starts to turn golden, 1 to 2 minutes. Add the salt, cayenne pepper, white pepper, and riced cauliflower. Decrease the heat to low and cook until the cauliflower is very soft and has turned golden yellow, 5 to 8 minutes.

Transfer the cauliflower mixture to a bowl, add the milk and eggs, and stir with a fork until blended.

In a large bowl, combine the fine corn flour, medium corn flour, potato starch, tapioca starch, baking powder, guar gum, and Parmesan and mix well. Add the cauliflower mixture and whisk quickly until just combined. Try not to stir the batter again after this.

Heat the æbleskiver pan over low to medium heat with ½ to 1 teaspoon of butter in each cavity. Using an ice cream scoop or a spoon, fill each cavity almost to the top.

Cook until a crust forms on the batter. Using a thin wooden skewer, turn the æbleskiver 90°, letting the batter spill over. Once a skin has formed, the æbleskiver will turn easily. Turn again in a different direction and then a last time to close up the sphere. Spin the æbleskiver around until evenly golden brown and cooked all the way through.

Preheat the oven to 400°F (200°C). Butter four 4-by-4-inch (10-by-10-cm) pans or one 9-by-13-inch (23-by-33-cm) oven-safe pan.

Place 3 or 4 æbleskiver in each of the small pans or place them all in the larger pan. Sprinkle with the shredded Cheddar cheese and bake for 8 to 10 minutes, or until golden brown. Remove from the oven and sprinkle with the crushed peppercorns.

TO SERVE: Garnish the æbleskiver with pieces of fresh cauliflower and micro greens (if using).

SWEET PEA ÆBLESKIVER
WITH FRIED GARLIC CHIPS

Makes about 21 æbleskiver | NF | VG

FRIED GARLIC CHIPS

¼ cup (60 ml) olive oil
or avocado oil

2 heads garlic, cloves peeled and
thinly sliced

ÆBLESKIVER

1¼ cups (150 g) fresh or frozen
peas

½ cup (120 ml) heavy cream

½ recipe Fried Garlic Chips,
crushed (above)

1 teaspoon salt

¼ teaspoon ground cardamom

Pinch of white pepper

2 cups (280 g) all-purpose flour

1 tablespoon sugar

2 teaspoons baking powder

½ teaspoon baking soda

2 cups (480 ml) milk

1 large egg

Reserved garlic oil from Fried
Garlic Chips (above)

Pea shoots and edible pea leaves
and flowers, for garnish (optional)

TO MAKE THE GARLIC CHIPS: Heat the oil in a small frying pan over medium-high heat. Lower the heat to medium-low, add the garlic slices, and cook, stirring, until they turn golden, 2 to 3 minutes.

Using a slotted spoon, transfer the garlic chips to sheets of paper towels. Reserve the oil in the frying pan to use in the æbleskiver batter.

Crush about half the garlic chips and save the rest to garnish the plates.

TO MAKE THE ÆBLESKIVER: In a saucepan over medium-high heat, combine 1 cup (120 g) of the peas and the cream and bring to a boil. Cook until thickened, about 15 minutes. Mash the peas, leaving a few whole. Remove from the heat and stir in the crushed garlic chips, salt, cardamom, and white pepper. Set aside.

In a large bowl, combine the flour, sugar, baking powder, and baking soda and mix well.

In a separate bowl, stir together the milk, egg, and reserved garlic oil until just combined. Pour the mixture over the dry ingredients and whisk quickly until just combined. Gently stir in the pea mixture. Try not to stir the batter after this.

Heat the æbleskiver pan over low to medium heat with ½ to 1 teaspoon of butter in each cavity. Using an ice cream scoop or a spoon, fill each cavity almost to the top.

Cook until a crust forms on the batter. Using a thin wooden skewer, turn the æbleskiver 90°, letting the batter spill over. Once a skin has formed, the æbleskiver will turn easily. Turn again in a different direction and then a last time to close up the sphere. Spin the æbleskiver around until evenly golden brown and a toothpick inserted into it comes out mostly clean. Serve right away or keep the æbleskiver warm in a 200°F (100°C) oven.

TO SERVE: Serve the æbleskiver warm and garnish with the remaining ¼ cup (30 g) of peas and the remaining fried garlic chips. Garnish with pea shoots and edible pea leaves and flowers (if using).

PURPLE SWEET POTATO ÆBLESKIVER
WITH PARMESAN ICE CREAM AND CHIPS

Makes about 21 æbleskiver | NF | VG

2 pounds (910 g) purple sweet potatoes

1 cup (240 ml) milk

1 teaspoon salt

¼ teaspoon ground white pepper

½ cup (50 g) grated Parmesan cheese

3 large eggs

1½ cups (210 g) all-purpose flour

¼ cup (45 g) potato starch

1 tablespoon baking powder

¼ cup (55 g) melted butter + more for the pan

Parmesan Ice Cream (page 117)

Parmesan Chips (page 117)

Microgreens, for garnish (optional)

Preheat the oven to 425°F (220°C).

Place the potatoes on a baking sheet, poke some holes in the skin with a fork, and bake for about an hour or until they're soft inside when pierced with a fork. Let the potatoes cool to room temperature.

Cut the potatoes in half and scoop out the flesh into a food processor. Add the milk, salt, and pepper and process until smooth. Pour the mixture into a large bowl and whisk in the cheese and eggs.

Add the flour, potato starch, and baking powder and stir until incorporated. Gently stir in the ¼ cup (55 g) of melted butter and try not to stir the batter again after this.

Heat the æbleskiver pan over low to medium heat with ½ to 1 teaspoon of butter in each cavity. Using an ice cream scoop or a spoon, fill each cavity almost to the top.

Cook until a crust forms on the batter. Using a thin wooden skewer, turn the æbleskiver 90°, letting the batter spill over. Once a skin has formed, the æbleskiver will turn easily. Turn again in a different direction and then a last time to close up the sphere. Spin the æbleskiver around until evenly golden brown and a toothpick inserted into it comes out mostly clean. Serve right away or keep the æbleskiver warm in a 200°F (100°C) oven.

TO SERVE: Serve the æbleskiver with the Parmesan ice cream and Parmesan chips. Garnish with micro greens (if using).

PARMESAN ICE CREAM

Makes about 5½ cups (1.2 k) | GF | NF | VG

2 cups (480 ml) cold heavy cream

1 cup (100 g) grated Parmesan cheese

One 14-ounce (400-ml) can sweetened condensed milk

Combine 1 cup (240 ml) of the cream and the Parmesan cheese in a pan over low heat. Cook, stirring, until the cheese has melted, 3 to 5 minutes.

Strain into a bowl for a silky smooth texture (discard the solids) and stir in the remaining 1 cup (240 ml) of cold cream. Refrigerate until completely cold.

Using an electric mixer, whisk the cream mixture until it reaches stiff peaks.

Carefully fold in the condensed milk and stir until blended only.

Pour the mixture into a freezer-safe container, cover, and freeze overnight.

PARMESAN CHIPS

Makes about 40 chips | GF | NF | VG

1 cup (100 g) shredded Parmesan, Parmesan Romano, or Pecorino Romano cheese

Preheat the oven to 350°F (180°C). Line a baking sheet with parchment paper.

Spoon 1 teaspoon of the cheese into rounds on the prepared baking sheet, about 1 inch (2.5 cm) apart.

Bake for 6 to 8 minutes, or until golden. Let cool.

BAMBOO RICE ÆBLESKIVER
WITH ROASTED HAZELNUTS AND FRESH HERB SAUCE

Makes about 14 æbleskiver | VG

FRESH HERB SAUCE

2 to 3 cups (24 to 36 g) fresh cilantro (about 1 bunch)

½ cup (6 g) fresh parsley

¼ cup (3 g) fresh mint

¼ cup (60 ml) grapeseed oil

½ cup (120 ml) buttermilk

½ cup (120 g) sour cream

Salt

ÆBLESKIVER

1 cup (140 g) roughly chopped hazelnuts

1 cup (140 g) all-purpose flour

1 cup (110 g) hazelnut flour

¼ cup (45 g) potato starch

1 tablespoon baking powder

½ teaspoon salt

2 tablespoons sugar

½ cup (120 ml) Fresh Herb Sauce (above)

1 cup (240 ml) buttermilk

2 large eggs

1 cup (180 g) cooked bamboo rice or other short-grain rice

¼ cup (35 g) cooked wild rice (optional)

¼ cup (55 g) melted butter + more for the pan

TO MAKE THE SAUCE: Set aside some of the fresh herbs for serving. Combine the remaining cilantro, parsley, and mint in a blender. Add the oil, buttermilk, and sour cream and process until smooth. Taste and season with salt as needed. Refrigerate until ready to serve.

TO MAKE THE ÆBLESKIVER: Preheat the oven to 350°F (180°C). Line a baking sheet with parchment paper.

Place the hazelnuts on the prepared baking sheet. Bake for 10 to 15 minutes, or until golden brown and fragrant. Rub the nuts in a towel to remove the skins. Let cool completely.

In a large bowl, combine the all-purpose flour, hazelnut flour, potato starch, baking powder, salt, and sugar and mix well. Set aside.

In a small bowl, combine half of the roasted hazelnuts and ½ cup (120 ml) of the herb sauce and mix well. Set aside.

In another bowl, lightly mix together the buttermilk, eggs, cooked bamboo rice, cooked wild rice (if using), and ¼ cup (55 g) of melted butter with a fork. Pour the mixture over the dry ingredients and whisk quickly until just combined. Gently fold in the herb and hazelnut mixture and try not to stir the batter again after this.

Heat the æbleskiver pan over low to medium heat with ½ to 1 teaspoon of butter in each cavity. Using an ice cream scoop or a spoon, fill each cavity almost to the top.

Cook until a crust forms on the batter. Using a thin wooden skewer, turn the æbleskiver 90°, letting the batter spill over. Once a skin has formed, the æbleskiver will turn easily. Turn again in a different direction and then a last time to close up the sphere. Spin the æbleskiver around until evenly golden brown and a toothpick inserted into it comes out mostly clean. Serve right away or keep the æbleskiver warm in a 200°F (100°C) oven.

TO SERVE: Pour some of the remaining herb sauce over the æbleskiver and serve the rest on the side. Sprinkle with the reserved fresh herbs and the remaining roasted hazelnuts.

CORNBREAD ÆBLESKIVER
WITH GUACAMOLE AND BLACK BEAN SALAD

Each recipe makes about 14 æbleskiver

CLASSIC CORNBREAD ÆBLESKIVER | NF | VG

1 cup (140 g) all-purpose flour

½ cup (70 g) medium-grind cornmeal

¾ cup (150 g) sugar

1 tablespoon baking powder

½ teaspoon salt

1 cup (240 ml) buttermilk

2 large eggs

1 cup (160 g) fresh corn

½ cup (30 g) finely chopped fresh chives

3 tablespoons melted butter + more for the pan

GLUTEN-FREE CORNBREAD ÆBLESKIVER GF | NF | VG

½ cup (70 g) sweet rice flour

¼ cup (35 g) brown rice flour

¼ cup (45 g) potato starch

½ cup (70 g) medium-grind cornmeal

¾ cup (150 g) sugar

1 tablespoon baking powder

1 teaspoon guar gum

½ teaspoon salt

1 cup (240 ml) buttermilk

2 large eggs

1 cup (160 g) fresh corn

½ cup (30 g) finely chopped fresh chives

3 tablespoons melted butter + more for the pan

VEGAN CORNBREAD ÆBLESKIVER | NF | V

1 cup (140 g) all-purpose flour

½ cup (70 g) medium-grind cornmeal

¾ cup (150 g) sugar

1 tablespoon baking powder

½ teaspoon salt

1 cup (240 ml) plant milk + 2 tablespoons fresh lemon juice, stirred together

½ cup (125 g) applesauce

1 cup (160 g) fresh corn

½ cup (30 g) finely chopped fresh chives

3 tablespoons oil + more for the pan

Guacamole (page 122), for serving

Black Bean Salad (page 123), for serving

TO MAKE EACH ÆBLESKIVER RECIPE: Mix together the dry ingredients in a large bowl and set aside.

In a separate bowl, lightly mix together the wet ingredients with a fork. Pour over the dry ingredients and whisk quickly until just combined. Try not to stir the batter again after this.

Heat the æbleskiver pan over low to medium heat with ½ to 1 teaspoon of butter or oil in each cavity. Using an ice cream scoop or a spoon, fill each cavity almost to the top.

Cook until a crust forms on the batter. Using a thin wooden skewer, turn the æbleskiver 90°, letting the batter spill over. Once a skin has formed, the æbleskiver will turn easily. Turn again in a different direction and then a last time to close up the sphere. Spin the æbleskiver around until evenly golden brown and a toothpick inserted into it comes out mostly clean. Serve right away or keep the æbleskiver warm in a 200°F (100°C) oven.

TO SERVE: Serve the æbleskiver warm with the guacamole and black bean salad.

GUACAMOLE

Makes about 2 cups (455 g) | GF | NF | V

3 ripe avocados, pitted and peeled

1 tablespoon fresh lime juice

Pinch of ground cayenne pepper

½ teaspoon salt

½ cup (70 g) finely chopped red onion

2 tomatoes, finely chopped

¼ cup (10 g) chopped fresh cilantro

1 jalapeño, seeded and finely chopped

2 garlic cloves, minced

In a medium bowl, mash together the avocado, lime juice, cayenne pepper, and salt. Fold in the onion, tomatoes, cilantro, jalapeño, and garlic. Cover and refrigerate or serve immediately.

BLACK BEAN SALAD

Serves 4 to 6 | GF | V

HERB VINAIGRETTE

¼ cup (60 g) **walnut champagne vinegar**

½ cup (60 g) **grapeseed oil**

1 small **garlic clove, minced**

2 tablespoons **finely chopped fresh cilantro**

Juice of 1 **orange**

1 tablespoon **fresh lime juice**

Salt and pepper

BLACK BEAN SALAD

2 ripe **avocados, pitted and peeled**

1 teaspoon **flaky sea salt + more as needed**

Juice of ½ **lime**

2 ears cooked **corn, kernels removed, or one 15-ounce (430-g) can, rinsed and drained**

1 cup (175 g) **halved cherry tomatoes**

One 15-ounce (430-g) can **black beans, rinsed and drained**

½ cup (20 g) **fresh micro cilantro or chopped fresh cilantro**

1 small **red onion, diced or thinly sliced**

TO MAKE THE VINAIGRETTE: In a small bowl, whisk together the vinegar, oil, garlic, cilantro, orange juice, and lime juice. Taste and season with salt and pepper as needed.

TO MAKE THE BLACK BEAN SALAD: Chop or slice the avocados. Transfer them to a medium bowl and toss with the salt and lime juice to coat.

Place the corn, tomatoes, beans, cilantro, and red onion in stripes across a serving platter and drizzle some dressing over the top.

Taste and sprinkle with flaky sea salt, as needed, just before serving. Serve the remaining dressing on the side.

ROASTED BEET ÆBLESKIVER
WITH FRESH HERBS AND MACADAMIA NUTS

Makes about 21 æbleskiver | VG

ROASTED BEETS
1 pound (455 g) beets

Vegetable oil

Salt

SAVORY BEET CHIPS
5 small beets, in a variety of colors, very thinly sliced

1 tablespoon vegetable oil

½ teaspoon salt

ÆBLESKIVER
1½ cups (210 g) all-purpose flour

1 tablespoon baking powder

1 teaspoon salt

8 ounces (230 g) Roasted Beets (above)

1½ cups (360 ml) milk

2 tablespoons butter + more for the pan

½ cup (70 g) finely chopped onion

3 large eggs

6 ounces (170 g) chopped roasted and salted macadamia nuts + more for serving

Sour cream, for serving

Chopped fresh herbs (such as tarragon, dill, or parsley), for serving

Flaky salt, for serving

TO MAKE THE ROASTED BEETS: Preheat the oven to 400°F (200°C).

Scrub the beets but leave the skin on. Coat the beets in oil, sprinkle with salt, and wrap in aluminum foil. Place the wrapped beets in a roasting pan and bake for 50 to 60 minutes, or until the beets are tender.

Let the beets cool and use your fingers to rub off the skins.

TO MAKE THE BEET CHIPS: Lower the oven temperature to 300°F (150°C). Line a baking sheet with parchment paper.

Place the sliced beets in a bowl with the oil and salt and toss until well coated. Using kitchen tongs, place the beet slices in a single layer on the prepared baking sheet. Bake for 20 minutes. Turn the slices and bake for another 20 minutes, or until the beets are light and crispy. Transfer to a wire rack to let the chips cool.

TO MAKE THE ÆBLESKIVER: Combine the flour, baking powder, and salt in a large bowl and mix well. Set aside.

Grate the 8 ounces (230 g) of roasted beets using the large side of a box grater. Place in a bowl, add the milk, stir to combine, and set aside.

Melt the 2 tablespoons of butter in a medium saucepan over low heat. Add the chopped onion and cook, stirring often, until soft, 8 to 10 minutes.

Add the onion mixture to the grated beets and mix well. Whisk in the eggs. Add the macadamia nuts and stir to combine. Pour the mixture over the dry ingredients and stir quickly until just combined. Try not to stir the batter again after this.

Heat the æbleskiver pan over low to medium heat with ½ to 1 teaspoon of butter in each cavity. Using an ice cream scoop or a spoon, fill each cavity almost to the top.

Cook until a crust forms on the batter. Using a thin wooden skewer, turn the æbleskiver 90°, letting the batter spill over. Once a skin has formed, the æbleskiver will turn easily. Turn again in a different direction and then a last time to close up the sphere. Spin the æbleskiver around until evenly golden brown and a toothpick inserted into it comes out mostly clean. Serve right away or keep the æbleskiver warm in a 200°F (100°C) oven.

TO SERVE: Serve the æbleskiver with the remaining roasted beets, beet chips, macadamia nuts, sour cream, fresh herbs, and flaky salt.

FRIED POTATO ÆBLESKIVER
WITH FETA AND FRIED SAGE

Makes about 21 large or 42 small (1½ to 1¾-inch/4 to 4.5-cm) æbleskiver | NF | VG

2 pounds (910 g) firm potatoes such as Yukon gold or red

Butter, for the pan

Vegetable oil, for the pan

½ teaspoon salt + more as needed

1 cup (75 g) fresh sage leaves

1½ cups (210 g) all-purpose flour

1 tablespoon baking powder

2 cups (480 ml) milk

2 large eggs

6 ounces (170 g) crumbled feta cheese + more for serving

3 tablespoons sage flowers (optional)

Fill a bowl with cold water. Scrub the potatoes with water. It's okay to peel them but not necessary. Thinly slice the potatoes and drop them immediately into the bowl of water.

In a large frying pan over medium heat, combine equal amounts of butter and oil, enough to generously coat the bottom of the frying pan. Adding oil to the butter will slightly raise the smoke point without sacrificing the butter flavor, which for this recipe makes a big difference. Pat dry the potatoes with paper towels. Fry the potatoes until soft in the middle and crispy around the edges, 15 to 20 minutes. Sprinkle the potatoes with salt, transfer to a plate, and keep warm until ready to serve.

In the same frying pan, combine more butter and oil if needed. Fry the whole sage leaves until crispy, about 1 minute. Transfer to paper towels to drain.

In a large bowl, combine the flour, baking powder, and ½ teaspoon of salt. Set aside.

In another bowl, lightly mix together the milk and eggs with a fork. Pour the mixture over the dry ingredients and whisk quickly until just combined. Gently fold in the crumbled feta cheese and try not to stir the batter again after this.

Heat the æbleskiver pan over low to medium heat with ½ to 1 teaspoon of butter in each cavity. Once the butter starts to bubble, place one or two slices of fried potato, depending on size, at the bottom of each cavity before adding enough batter to fill it almost to the top.

Cook until a crust forms on the batter. Use a thin wooden skewer to turn the æbleskiver 90°, letting the batter spill over. Turn again in a different direction and then a last time to close up the sphere. Spin the æbleskiver around until evenly golden brown and a toothpick inserted into it comes out mostly clean. Serve right away or keep the æbleskiver warm in a 200°F (100°C) oven.

TO SERVE: Serve the æbleskiver with the potato side up next to a generous serving of fried potatoes and fried sage leaves. Top with more feta cheese and edible sage flowers (if using).

HUSH PUPPY ÆBLESKIVER
WITH TWO DIPPING SAUCES

Makes about 14 large or 28 small (1½ to 1¾-inch/4 to 4.5-cm) æbleskiver | NF | VG

HOT PEPPER AND PINEAPPLE DIPPING SAUCE

1 large red bell pepper, cored, seeded, and roughly chopped

2 habanero chiles, cored, seeded, and roughly chopped

¾ cup (180 ml) pineapple juice

½ cup (120 ml) brown rice vinegar

2 cups (400 g) sugar

3 tablespoons potato starch

JALAPEÑO AND CHIVE DIPPING SAUCE

1 cup (240 ml) buttermilk

½ cup (120 g) mayonnaise

1 jalapeño pepper, cored, seeded, and roughly chopped

1 tablespoon fresh lemon juice

¼ cup (15 g) chopped fresh chives

Salt and pepper

ÆBLESKIVER

1 cup (140 g) fine-grind yellow cornmeal

1 cup (140 g) all-purpose flour

¼ cup (50 g) sugar

2 teaspoons baking powder

½ teaspoon baking soda

1 teaspoon salt

½ teaspoon cayenne pepper

½ teaspoon dried oregano

1 cup (240 ml) buttermilk

2 tablespoons vegetable oil + more for the pan

2 large eggs

1 jalapeño pepper, cored, seeded, and finely diced

¼ cup (25 g) finely chopped scallion

Butter, for the pan

TO MAKE THE HOT PEPPER AND PINEAPPLE DIPPING SAUCE: Combine the bell pepper, habanero chiles, ½ cup (120 ml) of the pineapple juice, the vinegar, and sugar in a blender or food processor and puree until smooth.

Pour the mixture into a saucepan over medium heat and bring to a boil. Remove the pan from the heat and skim off any foam that may have formed.

In a small bowl, mix together the potato starch and the remaining ¼ cup (60 ml) of pineapple juice. Pour the mixture into the saucepan, stirring continually, and bring back to a heavy boil. It should thicken almost immediately. Remove from the heat and let cool.

TO MAKE THE JALAPEÑO AND CHIVE DIPPING SAUCE: Combine the buttermilk, mayonnaise, jalapeño, and lemon juice in a blender or food processor and puree until smooth. Stir in the chives, taste, and season with salt and pepper as needed. Cover and refrigerate until ready to serve.

TO MAKE THE ÆBLESKIVER: In a large bowl, combine the cornmeal, flour, sugar, baking powder, baking soda, salt, cayenne pepper, and oregano and mix well. Set aside.

In another bowl, lightly stir together the buttermilk, 2 tablespoons of oil, and eggs with a fork. Pour the mixture over the dry ingredients and stir quickly until just combined. Gently fold in the jalapeño and scallion. Try not to stir the batter again after this.

Heat the æbleskiver pan over low to medium heat with ½ to 1 teaspoon of butter in each cavity. Using an ice cream scoop or a spoon, fill each cavity almost to the top.

Cook until a crust forms on the batter. Using a thin wooden skewer, turn the æbleskiver 90°, letting the batter spill over. Once a skin has formed, the æbleskiver will turn easily. Turn again in a different direction and then a last time to close up the sphere. Spin the æbleskiver around until evenly golden brown and a toothpick inserted into it comes out mostly clean. Serve right away or keep the æbleskiver warm in a 200°F (100°C) oven.

TO SERVE: Serve the æbleskiver warm with the two dipping sauces on the side.

ZUCCHINI ÆBLESKIVER
WITH ALMOND-CRUSTED ZUCCHINI FLOWERS

Makes about 14 large or 28 small (1½ to 1¾-inch/4 to 4.5-cm) æbleskiver | VG

WARM CHEESE SAUCE

1 cup (240 ml) half-and-half

1 cup (80 g) shredded sharp Cheddar cheese

½ cup (40 g) shredded mozzarella

Pinch of ground nutmeg

Salt and pepper

ALMOND-CRUSTED ZUCCHINI FLOWERS

12 zucchini flowers

4 ounces (115 g) mascarpone cheese

¼ cup (20 g) shredded mozzarella

¼ cup (25 g) grated Parmesan cheese

½ cup (45 g) super-fine almond flour

1 cup (140 g) all-purpose flour

¼ teaspoon salt

1 egg yolk

½ to 1 cup (60 to 120 ml) sparkling water

Vegetable oil, for frying

CONTINUED

TO MAKE THE CHEESE SAUCE: In a saucepan over medium heat, bring the half-and-half almost to a boil. Remove the pan from the heat and stir in the Cheddar and mozzarella cheeses until melted and smooth. Season with nutmeg and salt and pepper to taste. Set aside until ready to use.

TO MAKE THE ZUCCHINI FLOWERS: Remove the pistils from the flowers and clean out any debris that might be inside the flowers.

In a small bowl, mix the mascarpone, mozzarella, and Parmesan until smooth. Spoon about 2 teaspoons of the mixture into each blossom.

In a medium bowl, mix together the almond flour, all-purpose flour, and salt. Whisk in the egg yolk and some of the sparkling water and keep adding more water until it is the consistency that will coat the back of a spoon.

Heat the oil in a large frying pan over medium heat. Line a plate with paper towels. Dip the stuffed flowers into the batter, making sure they are well coated, and fry them, turning often, until golden. Drain on the paper towel–lined plate.

CONTINUED.

ZUCCHINI ÆBLESKIVER
CONTINUED

ÆBLESKIVER

3 tablespoons butter + more for the pan

½ cup (70 g) finely chopped onion

2 cups (300 g) grated zucchini + 1 or 2 whole zucchinis for serving

1 cup (90 g) almond flour

¾ cup (105 g) all-purpose flour

½ cup (50 g) grated Parmesan cheese + more for serving

½ teaspoon salt

1 tablespoon honey

1½ cups (360 ml) buttermilk

2 large eggs

TO MAKE THE ÆBLESKIVER: Melt 3 tablespoons of butter in a large frying pan over low heat. Add the onion and cook until translucent, 8 to 10 minutes.

Add the grated zucchini and let simmer over medium heat, stirring occasionally, until the mixture is reduced almost to a paste, about 20 minutes. Transfer the zucchini, including the oil, to a small bowl. Set aside.

Heat the almond flour in a dry pan over medium-high heat and stir constantly until it turns a slightly darker color and smells toasted. It will take only a few minutes. Transfer the toasted almond flour to a large bowl and mix in the all-purpose flour, Parmesan, and salt. Set aside.

In another bowl, stir together the honey, buttermilk, and eggs. Pour the mixture over the dry ingredients and mix until just blended. Gently fold in the zucchini mixture and try not to mix again after this.

Heat the æbleskiver pan over low to medium heat with ½ to 1 teaspoon of butter in each cavity. Using an ice cream scoop or a spoon, fill each cavity almost to the top.

Cook until a crust forms on the batter. Using a thin wooden skewer, turn the æbleskiver 90°, letting the batter spill over. Once a skin has formed, the æbleskiver will turn easily. Turn again in a different direction and then a last time to close up the sphere. Spin the æbleskiver around until evenly golden brown and a toothpick inserted into it comes out mostly clean. Serve right away or keep the æbleskiver warm in a 200°F (100°C) oven.

TO SERVE: Serve the æbleskiver with the zucchini flowers. Thinly slice the remaining raw zucchini using a cheese slicer. Roll up the individual slices and place on the plate for decoration. Sprinkle with Parmesan and serve the cheese sauce on the side.

SAUSAGE-FILLED ÆBLESKIVER
WITH FIVE KINDS OF MUSTARD

Makes about 14 æbleskiver | NF

CONTINUED

SAUSAGE WITH CRISPY BACON AND A SMOKY KICK

About 5 feet (1.5 m) sausage casings

8 ounces (230 g) bacon

2 pounds (910 g) boneless pork shoulder, well chilled

3 garlic cloves, minced

2 tablespoons sherry vinegar, ice cold

2 tablespoons honey

1 teaspoon pimentón de la vera picante

1 teaspoon cayenne pepper

Pinch of salt

CONTINUED

TO MAKE THE SAUSAGE: Preheat the oven to 400°F (200°C). Line a baking sheet with parchment paper. Line a plate with paper towels. Soak the sausage casings and rinse each one with warm water all the way through. Keep soaked in warm water until ready to use.

Place the bacon on the prepared baking sheet and bake for 15 to 20 minutes, or until crispy. Transfer the bacon to the prepared plate. Roughly chop the bacon and set aside.

Cut the pork into chunks and put it through a meat grinder into a large bowl.

Add the cooked bacon, garlic, vinegar, honey, pimentón, cayenne pepper, and salt to the pork, mix well, and quickly put it through the meat grinder a second time. Knead the meat mixture until it comes together in one sticky mass. Refrigerate for at least 1 hour.

Stuff the sausage casings rather loosely, leaving about 4 inches (10 cm) of casing on either end. Gently compress each one and use a needle or sausage pricker over the whole sausage on both sides to pop any air pockets.

Tie the links together to form a long loop or pinch, twist, and spin the sausages to make small sausage links. Leave uncovered in the fridge overnight.

Preheat the oven to 350°F (180°C). Arrange the sausages on a rimmed baking sheet and bake for 1 hour. Drain and flip the sausages. Turn the oven to broil and broil for 5 minutes. Flip again and broil for another 5 minutes.

Cut the sausage into fourteen ¾-inch (2-cm) pieces. In a large frying pan over medium-high heat, cook the sliced sausage, stirring often, to brown on all sides. Set aside

CONTINUED

SAUSAGE-FILLED ÆBLESKIVER
CONTINUED

ÆBLESKIVER

1 cup (140 g) all-purpose flour

½ cup (80 g) coarse-grind semolina

¼ cup (50 g) sugar

1 tablespoon baking powder

½ teaspoon salt

2 large eggs

1 cup (240 ml) milk

3 tablespoons melted butter + more for the pan

14 slices Sausage with Crispy Bacon and a Smoky Kick, ¾ inch (2 cm) wide (above) or store-bought

Variety of mustards (pages 136–137), for serving

Fresh watercress, for serving (optional)

TO MAKE THE ÆBLESKIVER: In a large bowl, combine the flour, semolina, sugar, baking powder, and salt and mix well. Set aside.

In another bowl, stir together the eggs, milk, and 3 tablespoons of melted butter. Pour the mixture over the dry ingredients and stir quickly until just combined. Try not to stir the batter again after this.

Heat the æbleskiver pan over low to medium heat with ½ to 1 teaspoon of butter in each cavity. Once the butter starts to bubble, use an ice cream scoop or a spoon to drop a dollop of batter into each cavity. Place a slice of sausage on top. Cover each cavity with more batter.

Cook until a crust forms on the batter. Use a thin wooden skewer to turn the æbleskiver 90°, letting the batter spill over. Turn again in a different direction and then a last time to close up the sphere. Spin the æbleskiver around until evenly golden brown and a toothpick inserted into it comes out mostly clean. Serve right away or keep the æbleskiver warm in a 200°F (100°C) oven.

TO SERVE: Serve the æbleskiver with a variety of mustards and garnish with watercress (if using).

TARRAGON AND BEER MUSTARD

Makes 1 cup (240 ml) | NF | VG

¼ cup (40 g) yellow mustard seeds
½ cup (120 ml) beer
2 tablespoons brown mustard seeds
2 teaspoons white wine vinegar
1 tablespoon honey
2 tablespoons finely chopped fresh tarragon

In a small bowl, combine the yellow mustard seeds and beer and let sit overnight.

Place the beer mixture in a blender and puree until smooth. Add the brown mustard seeds, vinegar, honey, and tarragon and blend until the brown seeds break but not until smooth. Transfer to a bowl, cover, and refrigerate overnight.

Spoon the mustard into sterilized jars, seal, and refrigerate for 2 weeks before using.

COARSE-GROUND SWEDISH MUSTARD

Makes 1 cup (240 ml) | NF | GF | V

¼ cup (40 g) yellow mustard seeds
¼ cup (40 g) brown mustard seeds
½ cup (120 ml) water
1 tablespoon white wine vinegar
2 tablespoons brown sugar
2 tablespoons vegetable oil
pinch of salt

In a saucepan over medium-high heat, combine the yellow and brown mustard seeds and the water and bring to a boil. Remove the pan from the heat and set aside to cool.

Remove about one-third of the mustard seeds and crush them in a mortar and pestle. Return the crushed mustard seeds to the pan over medium heat and add the vinegar, brown sugar, honey, oil, and salt. Stir until the sugar has melted and everything is well blended.

Spoon the mustard into jars, seal, and refrigerate for at least 2 days before using.

HABANERO-PINEAPPLE MUSTARD

Makes 1 cup (240 ml) | NF | GF | V

½ cup (80 g) yellow mustard seeds
½ cup (120 ml) pineapple juice
1 tablespoon red wine vinegar
2 tablespoons light brown sugar
1 teaspoon habanero powder
pinch of salt
2 tablespoons vegetable oil

In a small bowl, combine the mustard seeds and pineapple juice and let sit overnight.

Place the mustard seed and pineapple mixture in a blender and add the vinegar, brown sugar, habanero powder, salt, and oil. Puree until smooth.

Pour into sterilized jars, seal, and refrigerate for 2 weeks before using.

SMOOTH HONEY MUSTARD

Makes ¾ cup (180 ml) | NF | GF | VG

2 tablespoons honey
¼ cup (50 g) raw sugar
½ cup (120 ml) heavy cream
Pinch of salt
½ cup (40 g) Colman's dry mustard

In a saucepan over low heat, combine the honey, sugar, and heavy cream and bring to a boil. Remove the pan from the heat. Add the salt and mustard powder and whisk until smooth.

Pour into jars, seal, and refrigerate. This mustard can be eaten right away.

BRANDY-BUTTER MUSTARD

Makes 1¼ cups (300 ml) | NF | GF | VG

¼ cup (60 ml) apple juice
2 teaspoons white wine vinegar
3 tablespoons honey
Pinch of salt
**¼ cup (40 g) ground yellow
mustard seeds**
**1 tablespoon ground brown
mustard seeds**
**1 tablespoon ground black
mustard seeds**
2 tablespoons brandy
½ cup (110 g) butter

In a saucepan over medium heat, combine the apple juice, vinegar, honey, and salt and bring to a boil. Decrease the heat to medium-low, cover, and simmer for 10 minutes. Remove the pan from the heat and let cool.

Stir in the yellow, brown, and black mustard seeds and the brandy. Cover and refrigerate for 1 week.

Using an electric mixer, whisk in the butter until light and fluffy. Keep refrigerated.

ÆBLESKIVER WITH SWEET PEA HUMMUS
AND BEET DIP

Makes about 14 æbleskiver | V

BEET DIP

1 pound (455 g) beets

2 tablespoons olive oil + more as needed

Salt

1 cup (140 g) raw cashews

1 tablespoon fresh lemon juice

2 tablespoons maple syrup

2 tablespoons plain vegan yogurt

1 garlic clove, minced

SWEET PEA HUMMUS

1½ cups (180 g) cooked green peas

1½ cups (275 g) cooked chickpeas

¼ cup (3 g) fresh cilantro

2 tablespoons tahini

2 teaspoons fresh lemon juice

1 garlic clove, minced

2 tablespoons olive oil

Pinch of salt

ÆBLESKIVER

6 tablespoons garbanzo fava flour

6 tablespoons water

1½ cups (210 g) all-purpose flour

1 tablespoon baking soda

½ teaspoon salt

1¼ cups (300 ml) almond milk

2 tablespoons maple syrup

Zest and juice from ½ lemon

2 tablespoons oil + more for the pan

Petite watercress, for serving (optional)

Sprouted chickpeas, for serving (optional)

2 tablespoons sesame seeds (black or white or a mix of both), for serving

TO MAKE THE BEET DIP: Preheat the oven to 400°F (200°C). Scrub the beets. Coat the beets in oil, sprinkle with salt, and wrap them in aluminum foil. Place the wrapped beets in a roasting pan and bake for 50 to 60 minutes, or until the beets are tender.

Let the beets cool enough to handle and rub off their skins. The skin should peel away easily, or they need to cook longer. Cut into rough chunks.

In a small saucepan over medium-high heat, combine the cashews and lemon juice and enough water to cover the cashews. Bring to a boil and immediately remove the pan from the heat. Cover and let sit for 30 minutes.

Rinse the cashews and transfer them to a food processor or blender. Add the maple syrup, yogurt, garlic, and beets and process until smooth and creamy. Set aside until ready to serve.

TO MAKE THE SWEET PEA HUMMUS: In a food processor or blender, combine the green peas, chickpeas, cilantro, tahini, lemon juice, garlic, olive oil, and salt and process until smooth and creamy. Set aside until ready to serve.

TO MAKE THE ÆBLESKIVER: In a bowl, stir the garbanzo fava flour with the water until smooth and set aside. Combine the flour, baking soda, and salt in a medium bowl and mix well. Set aside.

In another bowl, combine the almond milk, maple syrup, lemon zest, lemon juice, 2 tablespoons of oil, and garbanzo fava mixture and mix well. Pour the mixture over the dry ingredients and whisk quickly until just combined. Try not to stir the batter again after this.

Heat the æbleskiver pan over low to medium heat with ½ to 1 teaspoon of oil in each cavity. Using a spoon, fill each cavity almost to the top.

Cook until a crust forms on the batter. Using a thin wooden skewer, turn the æbleskiver 90°, letting the batter spill over. Once a skin has formed, the æbleskiver will turn easily. Turn again in a different direction and then a last time to close up the sphere. Spin the æbleskiver around until evenly golden brown and a toothpick inserted into it comes out mostly clean. Serve right away or keep the æbleskiver warm in a 200°F (100°C) oven.

TO SERVE: Serve the æbleskiver warm with the sweet pea hummus and beet dip in two separate bowls on the side. Garnish with petite watercress and sprouted chickpeas (if using). Top with sesame seeds.

FRESH FIGS AND BLUE CHEESE ÆBLESKIVER

Makes about 14 æbleskiver | NF | VG

1½ cups (210 g) all-purpose flour

1 tablespoon baking powder

1 teaspoon salt

2 large eggs

½ cup (100 g) dark brown sugar

1 cup (240 ml) milk

2 tablespoons butter + more for the pan

3 ounces (85 g) chopped dried figs

4 ounces (115 g) crumbled blue cheese + more for serving

Fresh fig leaves, for garnish (optional)

Fresh figs, for serving

Combine the flour, baking powder, and salt in a large bowl and mix well. Set aside.

Using an electric mixer, whisk the eggs and brown sugar until light and fluffy.

Combine the milk and 2 tablespoons of butter in a small saucepan over medium heat and stir until the butter is melted.

Pour the egg mixture into the dry ingredients, followed by the warm milk and butter, and stir quickly until just blended. Gently stir in the dried figs and 4 ounces (115 g) of crumbled blue cheese until just combined. Try not to stir the batter again.

Heat the æbleskiver pan over low to medium heat with ½ to 1 teaspoon of butter in each cavity. Using an ice cream scoop or a spoon, fill each cavity almost to the top.

Cook until a crust forms on the batter. Using a thin wooden skewer, turn the æbleskiver 90°, letting the batter spill over. Once a skin has formed, the æbleskiver will turn easily. Turn again in a different direction and then a last time to close up the sphere. Spin the æbleskiver around until evenly golden brown and a toothpick inserted into it comes out mostly clean. Serve right away or keep the æbleskiver warm in a 200°F (100°C) oven.

TO SERVE: Serve the æbleskiver on a bed of fresh fig leaves (if using), with fresh figs, whole or sliced, and large chunks of blue cheese.

EGGPLANT ÆBLESKIVER
WITH HAZELNUT-CRUSTED EGGPLANT AND FIG DRESSING

Makes about 21 æbleskiver | VG

FIG DRESSING

1 cup (150 g) diced fresh figs
¼ cup (60 ml) walnut vinegar
¼ cup (60 ml) grapeseed oil
¼ cup (30 g) roasted hazelnuts
1 garlic clove, minced
Pinch of salt

HAZELNUT-CRUSTED EGGPLANT

2 eggs
1 cup (115 g) hazelnut flour
½ cup (50 g) finely grated Parmesan cheese
Pinch of salt
4 Japanese eggplants, cut into ⅛-inch (4-mm) slices
Vegetable oil, for the pan

ÆBLESKIVER

3 tablespoons butter + more for the pan
3 garlic cloves, minced
2 cups (500 g) peeled grated eggplant
1½ cups (210 g) all-purpose flour
1 cup (115 g) hazelnut flour
½ cup (50 g) grated Parmesan cheese
2 teaspoons baking powder
½ teaspoon baking soda
½ teaspoon salt
2 eggs
1½ cups (360 ml) buttermilk

Fresh watercress, for serving (optional)

TO MAKE THE DRESSING: Combine the figs, vinegar, grapeseed oil, hazelnuts, garlic, and salt in a food processor or blender and process until smooth and creamy. Set aside.

TO MAKE THE HAZELNUT-CRUSTED EGGPLANT: Line two plates with paper towels. Prepare two shallow bowls, one with lightly beaten eggs and one with the hazelnut flour, Parmesan, and salt, well mixed.

Dip the eggplant slices first in the eggs, then in the nut mixture.

In a large frying pan over medium heat, warm enough oil to generously coat the bottom of the frying pan. Add the eggplant slices in one layer and fry until golden and crispy, 4 to 5 minutes on each side. You may need to cook the eggplant in batches. Transfer the eggplant to the paper towel–lined plates.

TO MAKE THE ÆBLESKIVER: In a small frying pan over medium-low heat, melt the 3 tablespoons of butter. Add the garlic and cook until soft, 1 to 2 minutes. Add the grated eggplant and cook, stirring occasionally, for 10 minutes. Remove from the heat and let cool to room temperature.

In a large bowl, combine the all-purpose flour, hazelnut flour, Parmesan, baking powder, baking soda, and salt and mix well.

In another bowl, stir together the eggs, buttermilk, and cooked eggplant until just combined. Pour the mixture over the dry ingredients and whisk quickly until just combined. Try not to stir the batter again after this.

Heat the æbleskiver pan over low to medium heat with ½ to 1 teaspoon of butter in each cavity. Using an ice cream scoop or a spoon, fill each cavity almost to the top.

Cook until a crust forms on the batter. Using a thin wooden skewer, turn the æbleskiver 90°, letting the batter spill over. Once a skin has formed, the æbleskiver will turn easily. Turn again in a different direction and then a last time to close up the sphere. Spin the æbleskiver around until evenly golden brown and a toothpick inserted into it comes out mostly clean. Serve right away or keep the æbleskiver warm in a 200°F (100°C) oven.

TO SERVE: Place the warm æbleskiver on a bed of watercress (if using) with the hazelnut-crusted eggplant drizzled with the fig dressing.

QUAIL EGG ÆBLESKIVER
WITH TURMERIC AND AMARANTH

Makes about 14 æbleskiver | GF | NF | VG

14 quail eggs

½ cup (75 g) amaranth flour

½ cup (70 g) fine-grind yellow cornmeal

½ cup (70 g) medium-grind yellow cornmeal

3 tablespoons brown sugar

1 tablespoon baking powder

1 teaspoon guar gum

½ teaspoon salt

½ teaspoon ground turmeric

2 large eggs

1½ cups (360 ml) buttermilk

Butter, for the pan

A variety of amaranth greens, for garnish (optional)

Bring a pot of water to a boil over medium-high heat. Carefully drop the quail eggs into the boiling water and boil for 4 minutes. Let cool in cold water. Peel and refrigerate until ready to use.

Combine the amaranth flour, fine-grind cornmeal, medium-grind cornmeal, brown sugar, baking powder, guar gum, salt, and turmeric in a large bowl and mix well. Set aside.

In another bowl, lightly whisk together the eggs and buttermilk with a fork. Pour the mixture over the dry ingredients and whisk quickly until just combined. Try not to stir the batter again after this.

Heat the æbleskiver pan over low to medium heat with ½ to 1 teaspoon of butter in each cavity. Once the butter starts to bubble, use an ice cream scoop or a spoon to drop a dollop of batter into each cavity. Place 1 egg on top of each and push it down gently into the batter. Cover each cavity with more batter.

Cook until a crust forms on the batter. Using a thin wooden skewer to turn the æbleskiver 90°, letting the batter spill over. Turn again in a different direction and then a last time to close up the sphere. Spin the æbleskiver around until evenly golden brown and a toothpick inserted into it comes out mostly clean. Serve right away or keep the æbleskiver warm in a 200°F (100°C) oven.

TO SERVE: Garnish the æbleskiver with a variety of amaranth greens (if using).

TO MAKE THE SWEET HONEY DIPPING SAUCE (OPTIONAL): Mix in a bowl, ½ cup (120 g) mayonnaise; ½ cup (120 g) sour cream; ¼ cup (50g) brown sugar; 2 tablespoons lemon juice; 2 tablespoons Dijon mustard; Pinch of salt. Refrigerate until ready to use. Makes 1¼ cup | GF | NF | VG

HASHBROWN ÆBLESKIVER
WITH PICKLED BEETS, HORSERADISH MAYO, AND FRIED EGGS

Makes about 14 large or 28 small (1½ to 1¾-inch/4 to 4.5-cm) æbleskiver | GF | NF

PICKLED BEETS

1 pound (455 g) red beets of similar size, scrubbed

½ teaspoon salt

½ cup (120 ml) white vinegar

1 cup (240 ml) water

½ cup (100 g) sugar

1 teaspoon mustard seeds

10 whole white peppercorns

HORSERADISH MAYO

½ cup (120 g) mayonnaise

¼ cup (60 g) sour cream

2 tablespoons grated fresh horseradish

1 teaspoon Dijon mustard

Salt and pepper

ÆBLESKIVER

2 pounds (910 g) potatoes, finely shredded

1 yellow onion, finely shredded

2 tablespoons butter + more for the pan

¼ cup (45 g) potato starch

1 teaspoon salt

½ teaspoon freshly ground nutmeg

¼ teaspoon white pepper

4 large eggs

½ cup (120 g) sour cream

1 cup (240 ml) milk

14 ounces (400 g) smoked ham, for serving

4 to 6 fried eggs, for serving

¼ cup (15 g) finely chopped chives, for garnish

Flaky salt

Edible forget-me-not flowers, for garnish (optional)

TO MAKE THE PICKLED BEETS: Bring a large saucepan of water to a boil over medium heat. Add the beets and salt and cook until fork-tender, 30 to 40 minutes, depending on the size of the beets. Drain and let cool until you can handle them.

Peel the beets or rub off the skins with your hands. Cut the beets into slices and place them into 1 or 2 clean jars with lids.

In the same saucepan over medium-high heat, combine the vinegar, water, sugar, mustard seeds, and peppercorns and bring to a boil, stirring, until the sugar has dissolved. Remove from the heat and let cool slightly. Pour the warm liquid over the beets, seal with the lids, and refrigerate. Makes about 2½ cups (700 g).

TO MAKE THE HORSERADISH MAYO: In a bowl, mix together the mayonnaise, sour cream, horseradish, and mustard. Taste and season with salt and pepper as needed. Cover and refrigerate until ready to serve.

TO MAKE THE ÆBLESKIVER: Rinse the potatoes and onions well in cold water and squeeze out as much liquid as possible.

Melt 2 tablespoons of butter in a frying pan over medium-low heat. Add the onion and cook, stirring often, until soft, 8 to 10 minutes. Add the potatoes and cook, stirring, for 2 to 3 minutes. The potatoes should only be semi-cooked at this point.

Transfer the onion-potato mixture to a large bowl and stir in the potato starch, salt, nutmeg, and white pepper. Add the eggs, sour cream, and milk and mix well.

Heat the æbleskiver pan over low to medium heat with ½ to 1 teaspoon of butter in each cavity. Using an ice cream scoop or a spoon, fill each cavity almost to the top.

Cook until a crust forms on the batter. Using a thin wooden skewer, turn the æbleskiver 90°, letting the batter spill over. Once a skin has formed, the æbleskiver will turn easily. Turn again in a different direction and then a last time to close up the sphere. Spin the æbleskiver around until evenly golden brown and cooked all the way through. Serve right away or keep the æbleskiver warm in a 200°F (100°C) oven.

TO SERVE: Place the æbleskiver on a bed of sliced, smoked ham and serve with the pickled beets, horseradish mayo, and a fried egg. Sprinkle with chopped chives and flaky salt. Garnish with edible forget-me-not flowers (if using).

BULGUR AND CHANTERELLE ÆBLESKIVER
WITH ROSEMARY AND LINGONBERRIES

Makes about 14 large or 28 small (1½ to 1¾-inch/4 to 4.5-cm) æbleskiver | VG | NF

NO-COOK LINGONBERRY JAM

1 cup (150 g) fresh or frozen lingonberries or cranberries + more for serving

½ cup (100 g) sugar

ROSEMARY CHANTERELLES

16 ounces (450 g) fresh chanterelles

3 tablespoons butter

1 tablespoon chopped fresh rosemary

Salt and pepper

ÆBLESKIVER

6 ounces (180 g) cooked Rosemary Chanterelles (above)

¼ cup (10 g) chopped fresh parsley

¼ cup (35 g) dried lingonberries or cranberries

½ cup (40 g) grated sharp Cheddar cheese

¼ cup (45 g) potato starch

3 cups (420 g) cooked medium-grind bulgur

3 large eggs

Butter, for the pan

1 cup (12 g) micro parsley, for garnish (optional)

Fresh rosemary with edible rosemary flowers, for garnish (optional)

TO MAKE THE LINGONBERRY JAM: In a bowl, stir together the lingonberries and sugar until the sugar has completely dissolved. Cover and refrigerate until ready to use.

TO MAKE THE CHANTERELLES: Clean the chanterelles well and brush away any dirt.

In a large frying pan over high heat, cook the chanterelles and let the excess liquid evaporate, 5 to 10 minutes.

Lower the heat to medium, add the butter, rosemary, and salt and pepper to taste and continue to cook, stirring occasionally, until all the flavors are blended, about 5 minutes. Chop 6 ounces (180 g) of the chanterelles into ¼-inch (6-mm) pieces and reserve the rest for serving.

TO MAKE THE ÆBLESKIVER: In a medium bowl, mix together the chopped chanterelles, parsley, lingonberries, cheddar cheese, potato starch, bulgur, and eggs. Shape the mixture into balls big enough to fit the cavities of the æbleskiver pan.

Heat the æbleskiver pan over low to medium heat with ½ to 1 teaspoon of butter in each cavity. Fill each cavity with one of the balls.

Cook until a crust forms. Using a thin wooden skewer, turn the æbleskiver 90°, then turn again in a different direction. When the æbleskiver is holding together, turn a last time to close up the sphere. Spin the æbleskiver around until evenly golden brown and cooked all the way through. Serve right away or keep the æbleskiver warm in a 200°F (100°C) oven.

TO SERVE: Serve the æbleskiver on a bed of micro parsley (if using) and garnish with fresh rosemary, edible rosemary flowers (if using), and lingonberries. Serve with the remaining whole chanterelles and the lingonberry jam on the side.

CRANBERRY BACON ÆBLESKIVER
WITH ROASTED PECANS AND CRANBERRY SAUCE

Makes about 14 æbleskiver

ROASTED PECANS

1¼ cups (150 g) raw pecans

2 teaspoons grapeseed oil

2 teaspoons maple syrup

¼ teaspoon salt

CRANBERRY SAUCE WITH ROASTED PECANS

1 pound (455 g) fresh cranberries

8 ounces (230 g) dried cranberries

½ cup (120 ml) fresh orange juice + zest for garnish

1 cup (240 ml) maple syrup + more for serving

½ cup (60 g) Roasted Pecans (above)

ÆBLESKIVER

12 slices bacon, roughly chopped

2 tablespoons bacon fat

½ cup (70 g) dried cranberries

2 large eggs

2 cups (480 ml) milk

1½ cups (210 g) all-purpose flour

1 tablespoon baking powder

½ cup (60 g) Roasted Pecans (above)

Butter, for the pan

TO MAKE THE ROASTED PECANS: Preheat the oven to 350°F (180°C). Line a baking sheet with parchment paper.

In a bowl, combine the pecans, grapeseed oil, maple syrup, and salt and toss until well coated. Spread out the pecans on the prepared baking sheet. Bake for about 15 minutes, tossing the pecans halfway through, until they are fragrant and a shade darker. Chop and set aside.

TO MAKE THE CRANBERRY SAUCE: In a medium saucepan over medium heat, combine the fresh cranberries, dried cranberries, orange juice, and 1 cup (240 ml) of maple syrup and bring to a boil. Cook, stirring often, until the sauce thickens and the berries start to fall apart, about 20 minutes.

Remove the pan from the heat and stir in ½ cup (60 g) of roasted pecans. Let cool to room temperature. Set aside until ready to serve or refrigerate in an airtight container for up to 2 weeks.

TO MAKE THE ÆBLESKIVER: In a medium frying pan over medium heat, cook the bacon, stirring often, until crispy. Set aside about ¼ cup (about 50 g) of bacon for serving.

Transfer the remaining bacon with 2 tablespoons of the bacon fat to a large bowl. Stir in the dried cranberries, eggs, and milk. Add the flour and baking powder and whisk quickly until just combined. Gently fold in ½ cup (60 g) of roasted pecans. Try not to stir the batter again after this.

Heat the æbleskiver pan over low to medium heat with ½ to 1 teaspoon of butter in each cavity. Using an ice cream scoop or a spoon, fill each cavity almost to the top.

Cook until a crust forms on the batter. Using a thin wooden skewer, turn the æbleskiver 90°, letting the batter spill over. Once a skin has formed, the æbleskiver will turn easily. Turn again in a different direction and then a last time to close up the sphere. Spin the æbleskiver around until evenly golden brown and a toothpick inserted into it comes out mostly clean. Serve right away or keep the æbleskiver warm in a 200°F (100°C) oven.

TO SERVE: Serve the æbleskiver with the cranberry sauce and maple syrup. I like to serve them with roasted Brussels sprouts. Garnish with the remaining roasted pecans, reserved chopped bacon, and orange zest.

FRESH BASIL AND MOZZARELLA–STUFFED ÆBLESKIVER
WITH CHILE-LIME DRESSING

Makes about 14 æbleskiver | NF | VG

CHILE-LIME DRESSING

1 cup (240 ml) olive oil

¼ cup (60 ml) fresh lime juice

2 teaspoons honey

1 fresh Fresno red chile pepper, half finely chopped and half thinly sliced

1 fresh aji amarillo chile pepper, half finely chopped and half thinly sliced

2 tablespoons finely chopped fresh basil leaves

¼ teaspoon salt

ÆBLESKIVER

1½ cups (210 g) all-purpose flour

2 tablespoons sugar

2 teaspoons baking powder

½ teaspoon baking soda

½ teaspoon salt

2 cups (480 ml) buttermilk

2 large eggs

2 tablespoons melted butter + more for the pan

14 cherry-size mozzarella balls

14 fresh basil leaves

Edible basil flowers, for garnish (optional)

TO MAKE THE DRESSING: In a bowl, whisk together the olive oil, lime juice, honey, chiles, basil, and salt until emulsified. Taste and adjust the seasoning (more spice, honey, or salt) to your liking. Cover and refrigerate until ready to use.

TO MAKE THE ÆBLESKIVER: In a large bowl, mix together the flour, sugar, baking powder, baking soda, and salt and mix well.

In another bowl, lightly mix together the buttermilk, eggs, and 2 tablespoons of melted butter with a fork. Pour the mixture over the dry ingredients and whisk quickly until just combined. Try not to stir the batter again after this.

Heat the æbleskiver pan over low to medium heat with ½ to 1 teaspoon of butter in each cavity. Once the butter starts to bubble, use an ice cream scoop or a spoon to drop a dollop of batter into each cavity. Wrap each mozzarella ball in a fresh basil leaf and stuff each one into the batter, pushing it down lightly. Cover each cavity with more batter.

Cook until a crust forms on the batter. Using a thin wooden skewer to turn the æbleskiver 90°, letting the batter spill over. Turn again in a different direction and then a last time to close up the sphere. Spin the æbleskiver around until evenly golden brown and a toothpick inserted into it comes out mostly clean. Serve right away or keep the æbleskiver warm in a 200°F (100°C) oven.

TO SERVE: Serve the æbleskiver hot with the chile-lime dressing and garnish with different kinds of basil flowers (if using).

CHEESY CHORIZO ÆBLESKIVER
WITH HEIRLOOM TOMATO SALAD

Makes about 14 large or 28 small (1½ to 1¾-inch/4 to 4.5-cm) æbleskiver | NF

HEIRLOOM TOMATO SALAD

2 pounds (910 g) heirloom tomatoes, sliced

½ cup (120 ml) olive oil

¼ cup (60 ml) white wine vinegar

¼ cup (35 g) finely chopped red onion

2 tablespoons finely chopped fresh thyme

½ teaspoon salt

ÆBLESKIVER

4 tablespoons olive oil + more for the pan

1 garlic clove, finely minced

12 ounces (340 g) fully cooked Spanish-style chorizo, sliced

1 teaspoon finely chopped fresh thyme

2 large eggs

2 cups (480 ml) milk

½ cup (40 g) shredded mozzarella cheese

1½ cups (210 g) all-purpose flour

1 tablespoon baking powder

Garlic scapes, for garnish (optional)

TO MAKE THE TOMATO SALAD: Place the tomato slices on a serving plate or on individual plates.

In a small bowl, vigorously whisk together the olive oil, vinegar, onion, thyme, and salt until well blended. Drizzle the dressing over the tomatoes. Set aside until ready to serve.

TO MAKE THE ÆBLESKIVER: Heat 2 tablespoons of the oil in a small frying pan over low heat. Add the garlic and cook until soft, 1 to 2 minutes. Add the chorizo and thyme and stir until heated through.

Remove 1 cup (140 g) of chorizo and roughly chop. Keep the rest warm until ready to serve.

In a large bowl, stir together the chopped chorizo, eggs, milk, shredded mozzarella, and remaining 2 tablespoons of olive oil. Add the flour and baking powder and whisk quickly until just combined. Try not to stir the batter again after this.

Heat the æbleskiver pan over low to medium heat with ½ to 1 teaspoon of oil in each cavity. Using an ice cream scoop or a spoon, fill each cavity almost to the top.

Cook until a crust forms on the batter. Using a thin wooden skewer, turn the æbleskiver 90°, letting the batter spill over. Once a skin has formed, the æbleskiver will turn easily. Turn again in a different direction and then a last time to close up the sphere. Spin the æbleskiver around until evenly golden brown and a toothpick inserted into it comes out mostly clean. Serve right away or keep the æbleskiver warm in a 200°F (100°C) oven.

TO SERVE: Serve the æbleskiver with the reserved sliced chorizo and the tomato salad. Garnish with garlic scapes (if using).

PESTO ÆBLESKIVER
FILLED WITH LAMB MEATBALLS

Makes about 21 æbleskiver

PESTO

2 cups (50 g) fresh basil leaves + more for garnish

½ cup (60 g) toasted pine nuts

½ cup (50 g) shredded Parmesan cheese

1 garlic clove, peeled

1 tablespoon fresh lemon juice

¼ teaspoon salt

Pinch of white pepper

½ cup (120 ml) olive oil

LAMB MEATBALLS

8 ounces (230 g) ground lamb

1 egg

1 garlic clove, finely minced

1 teaspoon ground fennel

¼ teaspoon salt

2 tablespoons vegetable oil

ÆBLESKIVER

1 cup (140 g) all-purpose flour

1 cup (140 g) whole-wheat flour

1 tablespoon baking powder

1 tablespoon sugar

1½ cups (360 ml) milk

2 large eggs

½ cup (50 g) shredded Parmesan cheese

¼ cup (65 g) Pesto (above) or store-bought

Butter or oil, for the pan

TO MAKE THE PESTO: Combine 2 cups (50 g) of basil, pine nuts, Parmesan, garlic, lemon juice, salt, and white pepper in a food processor and process until smooth. With the food processor running, drizzle in the olive oil and process until combined. Transfer to a bowl, cover, and refrigerate until ready to serve.

TO MAKE THE MEATBALLS: In a bowl, combine the ground lamb, egg, garlic, fennel, and salt and mix well. Shape the mixture into about ¾-inch (2-cm) balls, or small enough to fit inside the cavities of the æbleskiver pan.

Heat the oil in a large frying pan over medium heat. Add the meatballs and cook, turning frequently, until golden brown on all sides, about 8 minutes. Remove from the pan, drain on paper towels, and set aside.

TO MAKE THE ÆBLESKIVER: In a large bowl, combine the all-purpose flour, whole-wheat flour, baking powder, and sugar and mix well. Set aside.

In another bowl, lightly stir together the milk and eggs with a fork. Pour the mixture over the dry ingredients and whisk quickly until just combined. Add the cheese and ¼ cup (65 g) of pesto and stir gently until combined. Try not to stir the batter again after this.

Heat the æbleskiver pan over low to medium heat with ½ to 1 teaspoon of butter in each cavity. Once the butter starts to bubble, use an ice cream scoop or a spoon to drop a dollop of batter into each cavity. Place a meatball on top and push it lightly into the batter. Cover each cavity with more batter.

Cook until a crust forms on the batter. Use a thin wooden skewer to turn the æbleskiver 90°, letting the batter spill over. Turn again in a different direction and then a last time to close up the sphere. Spin the æbleskiver around until evenly golden brown and a toothpick inserted into it comes out mostly clean. Serve right away or keep the æbleskiver warm in a 200°F (100°C) oven.

TO SERVE: Serve the æbleskiver warm with the pesto on the side. Garnish with a generous amount of fresh basil.

GARLIC PROSCIUTTO ÆBLESKIVER
WITH PROSCIUTTO CHIPS AND ROASTED GARLIC

Makes about 21 æbleskiver | NF

ROASTED GARLIC

6 heads garlic

Olive oil

PROSCIUTTO CHIPS

6 ounces (170 g) thinly sliced prosciutto

ÆBLESKIVER

1 cup (140 g) all-purpose flour

1 cup 50 g) wheat bran

½ cup (70 g) whole-wheat flour

1 tablespoon baking powder

1 teaspoon sugar

3 heads Roasted Garlic (above)

2 ounces (55 g) Prosciutto Chips (above)

2 large eggs

2 cups (480 ml) buttermilk

¼ cup (55 g) melted butter + more for the pan

½ teaspoon ground pink peppercorns, for garnish

4 to 6 branches of Peruvian pink peppercorns, for garnish (optional)

TO MAKE THE ROASTED GARLIC: Preheat the oven to 400°F (200°C).

Cut about ½ inch (12 mm) off the top of each head of garlic. Drizzle olive oil over the top and wrap each head in aluminum foil. Bake for 40 to 50 minutes, or until the garlic is soft and golden brown. Set aside.

TO MAKE THE PROSCIUTTO CHIPS: Lower the oven temperature to 350°F (180°C). Line baking sheets with parchment paper. You may need more than one.

Place the sliced prosciutto on the prepared baking sheets. Bake for 10 to 15 minutes, or until crispy. Set aside.

TO MAKE THE ÆBLESKIVER: Combine the all-purpose flour, wheat bran, whole-wheat flour, baking powder, and sugar in a large bowl. Set aside.

Squeeze the 3 heads of roasted garlic into a small bowl and stir until smooth. Crush the 2 ounces (55 g) of prosciutto chips and mix in with the garlic. Set aside.

In a separate bowl, lightly mix together the eggs, buttermilk, and ¼ cup (55 g) of melted butter with a fork. Pour the mixture over the dry ingredients and whisk quickly until just combined. Gently fold in the garlic/prosciutto mixture and try not to stir the batter again after this.

Heat the æbleskiver pan over low to medium heat with ½ to 1 teaspoon of butter in each cavity. Using an ice cream scoop or a spoon, fill each cavity almost to the top.

Cook until a crust forms on the batter. Using a thin wooden skewer, turn the æbleskiver 90°, letting the batter spill over. Once a skin has formed, the æbleskiver will turn easily. Turn again in a different direction and then a last time to close up the sphere. Spin the æbleskiver around until evenly golden brown and a toothpick inserted into it comes out mostly clean. Serve right away or keep the æbleskiver warm in a 200°F (100°C) oven.

TO SERVE: Serve the æbleskiver with the remaining prosciutto chips and roasted garlic. Garnish with ground pink peppercorns and branches of Peruvian pink peppercorns (if using).

BAKED PIZZA ÆBLESKIVER
WITH OLIVES AND PEPPERONI

Makes about 21 æbleskiver | NF

2 tablespoons olive oil + more for the pan

½ cup (70 g) finely chopped red onion

1 tablespoon honey

8 ounces (230 g) sliced mini pepperoni

2 tablespoons finely chopped fresh oregano

½ cup (70 g) sliced black olives

1 cup (140 g) all-purpose flour

1 cup (160 g) fine semolina flour

1 tablespoon baking powder

½ teaspoon salt

2 cups (480 ml) milk

2 large eggs

1 cup (80 g) shredded mozzarella cheese

Microgreens, for serving (optional)

Preheat the oven to 450°F (230°C).

Heat 2 tablespoons of oil in a frying pan over low heat. Add the chopped onion and cook until soft, about 5 minutes. Add the honey, 6 ounces (170 g) of the sliced pepperoni, and the oregano and cook over medium heat until the edges of the pepperoni start to crisp, about 5 minutes more. Stir in ¼ cup (35 g) of the black olives and set aside.

In a large bowl, combine the all-purpose flour, semolina flour, baking powder, and salt and mix well. Set aside.

In another bowl, stir together the milk, eggs, and ½ cup (40 g) of the mozzarella cheese. Pour the mixture over the dry ingredients and whisk quickly until just combined. Gently fold in the pepperoni and olive mixture, including the fat from the pan, and try not to stir the batter again after this.

Heat the æbleskiver pan over low to medium heat with ½ to 1 teaspoon of oil in each cavity. Using an ice cream scoop or a spoon, fill each cavity almost to the top.

Cook until a crust forms on the batter. Using a thin wooden skewer, turn the æbleskiver 90°, letting the batter spill over. Once a skin has formed, the æbleskiver will turn easily. Turn again in a different direction and then a last time to close up the sphere. Spin the æbleskiver around until evenly golden brown and a toothpick inserted into it comes out mostly clean.

Place the cooked æbleskiver in a large cast-iron frying pan or similar oven-safe pan. Top with the remaining ¼ cup (35 g) of olives, remaining 2 ounces (60 g) of pepperoni, and remaining ½ cup (40 g) of mozzarella and bake for 8 to 10 minutes, or until the cheese is completely melted and the pepperoni is getting crispy.. Serve right away or keep the æbleskiver warm in a 200°F (100°C) oven.

TO SERVE: Garnish the æbleskiver with the microgreens (if using).

SWISS CHARD ÆBLESKIVER
WITH PANCETTA AND FONTINA CHEESE

Makes about 14 æbleskiver | GF

2 tablespoons olive oil

1 garlic clove, finely minced

8 ounces (230 g) pancetta, diced

2 bunches Swiss chard, stems removed, leaves roughly chopped

Salt and pepper

1½ cups (180 g) fine almond flour

¼ cup (40 g) tapioca starch

2 teaspoons baking powder

1½ cups (360 ml) milk

3 large eggs

2 tablespoons melted butter + more for the pan

½ cup (60 g) shredded fontina cheese

Heat the oil in a large frying pan over medium heat. Add the garlic and pancetta and sauté until the pancetta is crackling, 3 to 4 minutes.

Add the Swiss chard leaves and sauté until the leaves are wilted, another few minutes. Taste and season with salt and pepper as needed. Set aside.

In a large bowl, add the almond flour, tapioca starch, and baking powder and mix well. Set aside.

In another bowl, lightly mix together the milk, eggs, and 2 tablespoons of melted butter with a fork. Pour the mixture over the dry ingredients and whisk quickly until just combined. Gently fold in 1 cup (100 g) of the cooked Swiss chard and pancetta mixture and the shredded cheese. Try not to stir the batter again after this.

Heat the æbleskiver pan over low to medium heat with ½ to 1 teaspoon of butter in each cavity. Using an ice cream scoop or a spoon, fill each cavity almost to the top.

Cook until a crust forms on the batter. Using a thin wooden skewer, turn the æbleskiver 90°, letting the batter spill over. Once a skin has formed, the æbleskiver will turn easily. Turn again in a different direction and then a last time to close up the sphere. Spin the æbleskiver around until evenly golden brown and a toothpick inserted into it comes out mostly clean. Serve right away or keep the æbleskiver warm in a 200°F (100°C) oven.

TO SERVE: Serve the æbleskiver warm with the remaining Swiss chard and pancetta mixture on the side.

BACON-WRAPPED ÆBLESKIVER
WITH BUTTER LETTUCE AND BLUE CHEESE DRESSING

Makes about 14 æbleskiver | GF | NF

BLUE CHEESE DRESSING

½ cup (120 g) sour cream

½ cup (120 g) mayonnaise

¼ cup (60 g) heavy cream

3 ounces (85 g) crumbled blue cheese + more for serving

2 teaspoons fresh lemon juice

Salt and pepper

ÆBLESKIVER

1 pound (455 g) sliced bacon

1 cup (90 g) cassava flour

½ potato starch (90 g)

¼ cup (30 g) tapioca starch

1 teaspoon guar gum

1 tablespoon baking powder

½ teaspoon salt

1 cup (240 ml) milk

2 large eggs

2 tablespoons mayonnaise

2 tablespoons maple syrup

2 tablespoons melted butter + more for the pan

4 to 6 fried eggs, for serving

Butter lettuce, for serving

TO MAKE THE DRESSING: In a bowl, mix together the sour cream, mayonnaise, heavy cream, 3 ounces (85 g) of blue cheese, and lemon juice. Taste and season with salt and pepper as needed. Cover and refrigerate until ready to use.

TO MAKE THE ÆBLESKIVER: Cut 10 bacon slices in half or into thirds, each about 4 inches (10 cm) long. Set aside.

Roughly chop the remaining bacon. In a frying pan over medium heat, cook the chopped bacon until crispy, 8 to 10 minutes. Set aside for serving.

In a large bowl, combine the cassava flour, potato starch, tapioca starch, guar gum, baking powder, and salt. Set aside.

In another bowl, lightly mix together the milk, eggs, mayonnaise, maple syrup, and 2 tablespoons of melted butter with a fork. Pour the mixture over the dry ingredients and whisk quickly until just combined. Try not to stir the batter again after this.

Heat the æbleskiver pan over low to medium heat with ½ to 1 teaspoon of butter in each cavity. Once the butter starts to bubble, arrange 2 slices of bacon in a cross pattern in each cavity and push them down to hug the sides. Using an ice cream scoop or a spoon, fill each cavity almost to the top with batter.

Cook until a crust forms on the batter. Use a thin wooden skewer to turn the æbleskiver 90°, letting the bacon slices follow the æbleskiver around and the batter spill over. Turn again in a different direction and then a last time to close up the sphere. Use the wooden skewer to keep the bacon tucked into the cavities. Spin the æbleskiver around until evenly golden brown and a toothpick inserted into it comes out mostly clean. Serve right away or keep the æbleskiver warm in a 200°F (100°C) oven.

TO SERVE: Serve the æbleskiver warm and top each serving with a fried egg. Serve with butter lettuce drizzled with the blue cheese dressing. Garnish with crumbled blue cheese.

MUSTARD AND DILL ÆBLESKIVER
WRAPPED IN SMOKED SALMON WITH CREAMY DIP

Makes about 21 æbleskiver | NF

CREAMY MUSTARD DIP

3 tablespoons coarse-ground Swedish mustard

1 tablespoon Dijon mustard

2 tablespoons honey

1 tablespoon white wine vinegar

1 cup (240 ml) grapeseed oil

½ cup (120 g) sour cream

¼ cup (3 g) finely chopped fresh dill

½ teaspoon salt

ÆBLESKIVER

2 cups (280 g) all-purpose flour

1 tablespoon baking powder

½ teaspoon salt

2 large eggs

1½ cups (360 ml) buttermilk

1 tablespoon Dijon mustard

½ cup (100 g) brown sugar

2 tablespoons fresh dill, finely chopped

¼ cup (55 g) melted butter + more for the pan

1 pound (455 g) smoked salmon

Edible mustard flowers, for garnish (optional)

TO MAKE THE DIP: In a medium bowl, whisk together the Swedish mustard, Dijon mustard, honey, and vinegar. Very slowly, pour the oil into the mixture and, with an electric mixer, vigorously whisk until well mixed and emulsified.

In a small bowl, mix together the sour cream, dill, and salt. Gently fold the mixture into the mustard sauce. Cover and refrigerate until ready to use.

TO MAKE THE ÆBLESKIVER: Combine the flour, baking powder, and salt in a large bowl and mix. Set aside.

In another bowl, lightly mix together the eggs, buttermilk, mustard, brown sugar, dill, and ¼ cup (5 g) of melted butter with a fork. Pour the mixture over the dry ingredients and stir quickly until just combined. Try not to stir the batter again after this.

Heat the æbleskiver pan over low to medium heat with ½ to 1 teaspoon of butter in each cavity. Using an ice cream scoop or a spoon, fill each cavity almost to the top.

Cook until a crust forms on the batter. Using a thin wooden skewer, turn the æbleskiver 90°, letting the batter spill over. Once a skin has formed, the æbleskiver will turn easily. Turn again in a different direction and then a last time to close up the sphere. Spin the æbleskiver around until evenly golden brown and a toothpick inserted into it comes out mostly clean. Serve right away or keep the æbleskiver warm in a 200°F (100°C) oven.

TO SERVE: Wrap each æbleskiver in a slice of smoked salmon and serve with the creamy mustard dip. Garnish with edible mustard flowers (if using).

POTATO CROQUETTE ÆBLESKIVER
WITH BACON, BAKED PEARS, AND WHISKEY

Makes about 21 æbleskiver | GF | NF

BAKED PEARS IN HONEY WHISKEY BUTTER

3 tablespoons butter

2 tablespoons honey

3 tablespoons whiskey

4 Bosc pears

ÆBLESKIVER

2½ pounds (1.2 kg) russet potatoes, peeled and cubed

½ cup (90 g) potato starch

2 large egg yolks

2 teaspoons salt

¼ cup (55 g) melted butter + more for the pan

1 pound (450 g) thick-cut bacon, cut into ¼-inch (6-mm) pieces

1 yellow onion, cut into ¼-inch (6-mm) pieces

¼ teaspoon grated nutmeg

1 teaspoon black pepper

TO MAKE THE BAKED PEARS: Preheat the oven to 350°F (180°C).

Combine the butter and honey in a saucepan over medium heat and stir until melted. Remove from the heat and stir in the whiskey. Set aside.

Peel the pears. Cut off the bases to make them stand up straight but keep the stems on. Stand the pears in an oven-safe dish and pour half the whiskey butter over the tops. Bake for 30 minutes. Pour the remaining whiskey butter over the pears and bake for another 30 minutes. The pears should be soft but still hold together. Remove from the oven and coat the pears with butter from the pan a few more times. Save the butter in a small bowl to serve on the side.

TO MAKE THE ÆBLESKIVER: Place the potatoes in a large pot, cover with salted water, and bring to a boil over medium-high heat. Lower the heat to medium and cook until the potatoes are tender, about 20 minutes.

Put the cooked potatoes through a ricer or mash them in a bowl. Add the potato starch, egg yolks, salt, and ¼ cup (55 g) of melted butter. Mix until smooth.

Combine the bacon and onion in a frying pan over medium heat and sauté until golden brown, 10 to 15 minutes. Stir in the nutmeg and the pepper. Reserve about ¼ cup (50 g) of the bacon mixture in a small bowl for serving. Set the rest aside.

Using an ice cream scoop or a spoon, scoop out enough mashed potato to almost fill one cavity of the pan. Use your hands to fill each potato scoop with 1 tablespoon of the bacon mixture and shape into a sphere, completely covering the bacon. Each sphere should fit the cavity of a large æbleskiver pan.

Bring a large pot of salted water to a boil. Boil a few croquettes at a time until they pop up to the surface, 5 to 6 minutes. Remove with a slotted spoon, place on a cooling rack, and let cool slightly.

Heat the æbleskiver pan over low to medium heat with ½ to 1 teaspoon of butter in each cavity. Once the butter starts to bubble, place one croquette in each cavity.

Cook until the edges are getting crispy. Use a thin wooden skewer to spin the æbleskiver around until evenly golden brown. Serve right away or keep the æbleskiver warm in a 200°F (100°C) oven.

TO SERVE: Serve the æbleskiver croquettes with the baked pears, honey whiskey butter, and a sprinkling of the reserved bacon mixture.

SAFFRON RICE ÆBLESKIVER
WITH SEAFOOD PAELLA

Makes about 21 æbleskiver | NF

SEAFOOD PAELLA

2 tablespoons vegetable oil

1 garlic clove, minced

½ cup (70 g) finely chopped onion

1 cup (200 g) bomba paella rice

Pinch of saffron threads

2 tablespoons finely chopped Italian flat-leaf parsley + more for garnish

¾ teaspoon salt

¼ teaspoon ground white pepper

2 cups (480 ml) fish stock or chicken stock

½ cup (60 g) finely chopped red bell pepper

½ cup (60 g) green peas

8 ounces (230 g) fully cooked medium shrimp, peeled and deveined

8 ounces (230 g) mussels, cleaned and cooked, with or without shells

½ cup (120 ml) white wine

½ teaspoon smoked paprika

ÆBLESKIVER

1½ cups (210 g) all-purpose flour

1 tablespoon baking powder

2 large eggs

2 cups (480 ml) milk

1 tablespoon vegetable oil + more for the pan

TO MAKE THE SEAFOOD PAELLA: Heat the oil in a heavy pot over medium heat. Add the garlic and onion and sauté for about 10 minutes.

Add the rice, saffron, 2 tablespoons of parsley, ½ teaspoon of the salt, and pepper and cook, stirring constantly, for a few minutes until everything is evenly coated. Pour in the stock and stir to combine. Cover and let simmer, without stirring, until the rice is al dente and the liquid is absorbed, 15 to 20 minutes.

Stir in the red pepper and green peas. Set aside 1 cup (200 g) of the saffron rice in a medium bowl for the æbleskiver batter and leave the rest in the pot.

Add the shrimp, mussels, wine, paprika, and remaining ¼ teaspoon of salt and stir to combine. Leave on very low heat until ready to serve.

TO MAKE THE ÆBLESKIVER: In a large bowl, combine the flour and baking powder and mix well.

In another bowl, lightly mix together the eggs, milk, and 1 tablespoon of oil with a fork. Pour the mixture over the dry ingredients and stir quickly until just combined. Gently stir in the reserved saffron rice. Try not to stir the batter again after this.

Heat the æbleskiver pan over low to medium heat with ½ to 1 teaspoon of oil in each cavity. Using an ice cream scoop or a spoon, fill each cavity almost to the top.

Cook until a crust forms on the batter. Using a thin wooden skewer, turn the æbleskiver 90°, letting the batter spill over. Once a skin has formed, the æbleskiver will turn easily. Turn again in a different direction and then a last time to close up the sphere. Spin the æbleskiver around until evenly golden brown and a toothpick inserted into it comes out mostly clean. Serve right away or keep the æbleskiver warm in a 200°F (100°C) oven.

TO SERVE: Serve the æbleskiver warm over a generous serving of seafood paella. Garnish with parsley.

WASABI EDAMAME ÆBLESKIVER
WITH POKE TUNA AND SRIRACHA MAYO

Makes about 21 large or 42 small (1½ to 1¾-inch/4 to 4.5-cm) æbleskiver | NF

SRIRACHA MAYO

1 cup (240 g) mayonnaise

3 tablespoons sriracha

1 tablespoon fresh lemon juice

1 garlic clove, finely minced

POKE TUNA

12 ounces (340 g) sushi-grade tuna, cut into ¼-inch (6-mm) cubes

1 teaspoon toasted sesame oil

1 teaspoon soy sauce

1 fresh mango, pitted, peeled, and diced

1 avocado, pitted, peeled, and diced

¼ cup (35 g) shelled edamame

¼ cup (12 g) chopped scallion

¼ cup (40 g) chopped cucumber

1 tablespoon black sesame seeds + more for garnish

ÆBLESKIVER

1 cup (160 g) shelled edamame

2 cups (480 ml) milk

2 tablespoons wasabi paste

2 tablespoons mayonnaise

1 tablespoon honey

2 large eggs

1½ cups (210 g) all-purpose flour

2 teaspoons baking powder

½ teaspoon salt

¼ cup (25 g) chopped scallion + more for garnish

Oil, for the pan

TO MAKE THE SRIRACHA MAYO: In a small bowl, add the mayonnaise, sriracha, lemon juice, and garlic and whisk until well combined. Cover and refrigerate until ready to serve.

TO MAKE THE POKE: In a bowl, combine the tuna cubes, sesame oil, and soy sauce and toss until well coated. Fold in the mango, avocado, edamame, scallion, and cucumber. Sprinkle 1 tablespoon of black sesame seeds over the top and refrigerate until ready to use.

TO MAKE THE ÆBLESKIVER: Combine the edamame and milk in a food processor and process until the edamame are a bit broken up but not completely pureed.

In a large bowl, whisk together the wasabi paste, mayonnaise, and honey until smooth. Add the eggs and stir until blended. Add the mixture to the edamame mixture and mix well.

In another bowl, combine the flour, baking powder, and salt and mix well. Add the mixture to the wet ingredients and whisk quickly until just combined. Gently fold in ¼ cup (25 g) of chopped scallion and try not to stir the batter again after this.

Heat the æbleskiver pan over low to medium heat with ½ to 1 teaspoon of oil in each cavity. Using an ice cream scoop or a spoon, fill each cavity almost to the top.

Cook until a crust forms on the batter. Using a thin wooden skewer, turn the æbleskiver 90°, letting the batter spill over. Once a skin has formed, the æbleskiver will turn easily. Turn again in a different direction and then a last time to close up the sphere. Spin the æbleskiver around until evenly golden brown and a toothpick inserted into it comes out mostly clean. Serve right away or keep the æbleskiver warm in a 200°F (100°C) oven.

TO SERVE: Place the æbleskiver on a serving platter or on individual plates. Spoon the poke tuna on top. Top with the sriracha mayo, chopped scallion, and a scattering of black sesame seeds.

CARROT WALNUT ÆBLESKIVER
WITH DILL-CURED SALMON AND CABBAGE SALAD

Makes about 21 æbleskiver

1 cup (140 g) all-purpose flour

½ cup (55 g) dark rye flour

1 tablespoon baking powder

½ teaspoon salt

2 cups (230 g) grated carrot

2 large eggs

1 cup (240 ml) buttermilk

¼ cup (60 ml) maple syrup

2 tablespoons vegetable oil

½ cup (60 g) chopped walnuts + extra for garnish

Butter, for the pan

Cabbage Salad (page 177), for serving

Thinly sliced Gravlax (page 176), for serving

Grated lemon zest, for garnish

Black sesame seeds, for garnish

Combine the all-purpose flour, rye flour, baking powder, and salt in a large bowl. Set aside.

In a separate bowl, stir together the grated carrot, eggs, buttermilk, maple syrup, and oil until combined. Pour the carrot mixture over the dry ingredients and whisk quickly until just combined. Gently stir in the walnuts and try not to stir the batter again after this.

Heat the æbleskiver pan over low to medium heat with ½ to 1 teaspoon of butter in each cavity. Using an ice cream scoop or a spoon, fill each cavity almost to the top.

Cook until a crust forms on the batter. Using a thin wooden skewer, turn the æbleskiver 90°, letting the batter spill over. Once a skin has formed, the æbleskiver will turn easily. Turn again in a different direction and then a last time to close up the sphere. Spin the æbleskiver around until evenly golden brown and a toothpick inserted into it comes out mostly clean. Serve right away or keep the æbleskiver warm in a 200°F (100°C) oven.

TO SERVE: Arrange the cabbage salad on individual plates. Add the æbleskiver and sliced gravlax to the plate and garnish with lemon zest and black sesame seeds.

GRAVLAX (CURED SALMON)

Makes 1½ to 2 pounds (680 to 910 g) | GF | NF

1 to 2 large bunches fresh dill

½ cup (70 g) coconut palm sugar

¼ cup (50 g) salt

6 tablespoons yellow mustard seeds

3 tablespoons pink peppercorns

1½ to 2 pounds (680 to 910 g) fresh salmon with skin, cleaned and bones removed

Sprinkle one-third each of the dill, sugar, salt, mustard seeds, and peppercorns on a large piece of aluminum foil. Place half the salmon on top. Sprinkle another one-third each of the dill, sugar, salt, mustard seeds, and peppercorns over the salmon. Add the remaining salmon, and top with the remaining dill and spices. Wrap tightly in the aluminum foil.

Place the foil package in a container with a lid or in a bowl covered with plastic wrap and refrigerate. Turn over the package twice a day for 2 to 3 days depending on how cured you want it. It will be milder after 2 days, almost like a mix between gravlax and sashimi, and take on more of the curing flavors after 3 days, which will be closer in flavor to store-bought gravlax.

Rinse the salmon under cold water and pat dry with paper towels. Place in an airtight container and refrigerate until ready to use.

Shortly before serving, slice the chilled salmon using a knife with a long, flexible blade. Starting at a 45° angle, cut toward the tail end, pushing the knife down and away to create large, thin slices. Continue to cut down the side of the salmon, angling the blade more and more until almost parallel to the counter. Serve cold.

CABBAGE SALAD

Serves 4 to 6 | GF | VG

3 cups (180 g) shredded
red cabbage

1 avocado, pitted, peeled, and diced

2 tablespoons minced shallot

4 radishes, thinly sliced

¼ cup (60 ml) fresh orange juice

¼ cup (60 ml) grapeseed oil

3 tablespoons balsamic vinegar

1 tablespoon honey

2 teaspoons fresh lemon juice

Salt and pepper

1 cup (45 g) mixed greens,
for serving

2 tablespoons sesame seeds,
for garnish

¼ cup (10 g) fresh edible dill
flowers, for garnish (optional)

In a bowl, combine the cabbage, avocado, shallot, and radishes and toss until well mixed. Cover and refrigerate until ready to serve.

In a small bowl, combine the orange juice, grapeseed oil, balsamic, honey, and lemon juice and stir until well blended. Taste and season with salt and pepper as needed.

Just before serving, pour the orange dressing over the cabbage salad and toss until well coated.

Divide the mixed greens onto plates and arrange the cabbage mixture on top. Garnish with sesame seeds and edible dill flowers (if using).

CASSAVA ÆBLESKIVER
STUFFED WITH SALMON, SPINACH, AND THYME

Makes about 21 large or 42 small (1½ to 1¾-inch/4 to 4.5-cm) æbleskiver | GF | NF

SALMON, SPINACH, AND THYME FILLING

2 tablespoons butter

2 cups (40 g) fresh spinach

1 garlic clove, finely minced

¼ cup (35 g) finely chopped onion

2 teaspoons fresh thyme leaves + more for garnish

¼ cup (60 ml) heavy cream

4 ounces (115 g) fresh salmon, finely chopped

¼ cup (25 g) grated Parmesan cheese

ÆBLESKIVER

12 ounces (340 g) peeled and cubed cassava/yucca root

1½ teaspoons salt

2 tablespoons melted butter + more for the pan

½ cup (120 ml) milk

½ cup (50 g) shaved Parmesan cheese + more for serving

½ cup (80 g) tapioca starch

2 teaspoons baking powder

1 recipe Salmon, Spinach, and Thyme Filling (above)

2 cups (90 g) mixed greens, for serving

TO MAKE THE SALMON FILLING: Melt 1 tablespoon of the butter in a frying pan over low heat. Add the spinach and cook, stirring constantly, until it wilts, about 1 minute. Place the spinach on a paper towel and squeeze out any excess liquid. Finely chop the spinach and set aside.

Melt the remaining 1 tablespoon of butter in the same frying pan over low heat. Add the garlic and onion and cook, stirring often, until the onion turns translucent, 8 to 10 minutes. Add the spinach, 2 teaspoons of thyme, and cream and cook until creamy, about 10 minutes.

Add the salmon and cook, stirring constantly, for about 1 minute. Remove the pan from the heat and stir in the cheese until blended. Set aside.

TO MAKE THE ÆBLESKIVER: In a saucepan over medium-low heat, combine the cassava root and 1 teaspoon of the salt, cover completely with water, and bring to a boil. Cook until the cassava is completely tender and easy to mash with a fork, about 20 minutes.

Drain the liquid and press the cassava through a potato ricer into a large bowl. Add 2 tablespoons of melted butter and the milk and beat with an electric mixer until smooth, light, and fluffy. Add ½ cup (50 g) of Parmesan cheese, the tapioca starch, baking powder, and remaining ½ teaspoon of salt and stir until a soft dough is formed.

Pinch out enough dough to fit the cavity of a large æbleskiver cavity. Make a dent in the middle and fill with 1 tablespoon of the salmon mixture. Shape into spheres.

Heat the æbleskiver pan over low to medium heat with ½ to 1 teaspoon of butter in each cavity. Once the butter starts to bubble, drop in the cassava balls and cook, using a thin wooden skewer to turn them until they are golden brown all over, 8 to 10 minutes. Serve right away or keep the æbleskiver warm in a 200°F (100°C) oven.

TO SERVE: Serve the æbleskiver on a bed of mixed greens, topped with fresh thyme and shaved Parmesan cheese.

SHRIMP ÆBLESKIVER
WITH SUN-DRIED TOMATOES AND BURNT BUTTER

Makes about 14 æbleskiver | NF

SUN-DRIED TOMATOES

2 cups (320 g) fresh cherry tomatoes, halved

Salt

BURNT BUTTER

1 cup (220 g) butter

ÆBLESKIVER

3 large eggs, separated

16 ounces (455 g) fully cooked, peeled, and deveined small-medium shrimp

¼ cup (55 g) butter + more for the pan

1 teaspoon anchovy paste

½ cup (120 ml) milk

1 cup (240 ml) heavy cream

¾ cup (105 g) all-purpose flour

2 teaspoons baking powder

1 teaspoon salt

Pinch of white pepper

TO MAKE THE SUN-DRIED TOMATOES: Preheat the oven to 175°F (80°C). Line a baking sheet with parchment paper.

Arrange the tomatoes, skin side down, on the prepared baking sheet. Sprinkle with salt. Bake, turning the baking sheet occasionally so they dry evenly, for 4 to 5 hours, or until leathery but still soft. Let cool.

The dried tomatoes can be stored in a zip-top plastic bag or you can pack them into a jar and cover with oil, fresh herbs, and a touch of vinegar. Place in an airtight container and refrigerate for up to 4 weeks.

TO MAKE THE BURNT BUTTER: In a heavy-bottomed pan over medium-low heat, melt the butter. Continuously swirl the butter around the pan and watch it closely as it begins to foam. The color will quickly go from yellow to golden tan to dark amber. As soon as it turns dark amber and smells nutty, remove the pan from the heat. Set aside.

TO MAKE THE ÆBLESKIVER: In a bowl using an electric mixer, beat the egg whites until firm peaks form. Set aside.

Combine 10 ounces (280 g) of the shrimp, ¼ cup (55 g) of melted butter, and the anchovy paste in a food processor and blend until smooth. Add the egg yolks, milk, and cream and process until blended. Pour the mixture into a large bowl.

Add the flour, baking powder, salt, and pepper to the bowl and whisk quickly until just combined. Gently fold in the beaten egg whites and try not to stir the batter again after this.

Heat the æbleskiver pan over low to medium heat with ½ to 1 teaspoon of butter in each cavity. Using an ice cream scoop or a spoon, fill each cavity almost to the top.

Cook until a crust forms on the batter. Using a thin wooden skewer, turn the æbleskiver 90°, letting the batter spill over. Once a skin has formed, the æbleskiver will turn easily. Turn again in a different direction and then a last time to close up the sphere. Spin the æbleskiver around until evenly golden brown and a toothpick inserted into it comes out mostly clean. Serve right away or keep the æbleskiver warm in a 200°F (100°C) oven.

TO SERVE: Serve the æbleskiver with the remaining 6 ounces (170 g) of shrimp, sun-dried tomatoes, and warm burnt butter.

BUCKWHEAT ÆBLESKIVER
WITH CRÈME FRAÎCHE AND CAVIAR

Makes about 21 æbleskiver | NF

1¼ cups (175 g) all-purpose flour

½ cup (70 g) buckwheat flour

2 teaspoons baking powder

½ teaspoon salt

2 large eggs

1½ cups (360 ml) milk

1 tablespoon sugar

2 tablespoons melted butter + more for the pan

¼ cup (35 g) finely chopped red onion, for serving

1½ cups (360 g) sour cream, for serving

1 small bunch fresh dill, for serving

3 small jars caviar in different colors, for serving

Combine the all-purpose flour, buckwheat flour, baking powder, and salt in a large bowl and mix well. Set aside.

In a separate bowl, lightly stir together the eggs, milk, sugar, and 2 tablespoons of melted butter. Pour the mixture over the dry ingredients and stir quickly until just combined. Try not to stir again after this.

Heat the æbleskiver pan over low to medium heat with ½ to 1 teaspoon of butter in each cavity. Using an ice cream scoop or a spoon, fill each cavity almost to the top.

Cook until a crust forms on the batter. Using a thin wooden skewer, turn the æbleskiver 90°, letting the batter spill over. Once a skin has formed, the æbleskiver will turn easily. Turn again in a different direction and then a last time to close up the sphere. Spin the æbleskiver around until evenly golden brown and a toothpick inserted into it comes out mostly clean. Serve right away or keep the æbleskiver warm in a 200°F (100°C) oven.

TO SERVE: Serve the æbleskiver lukewarm with finely chopped red onion, sour cream, fresh dill, and caviar.

CHARCOAL AND OCTOPUS ÆBLESKIVER
WITH BEET-PICKLED ONION AND SAFFRON AIOLI

Makes about 14 æbleskiver | NF

BEET-COOKED OCTOPUS

One 2-pound (910-g) whole octopus

1 red beet, scrubbed

Vegetable oil

Salt and pepper

ÆBLESKIVER

1½ cups (210 ml) all-purpose flour

2 tablespoons food-grade activated charcoal powder

2 teaspoons baking powder

½ teaspoon salt

2 cups (480 ml) vegetable stock

2 large eggs

1 cup (100 g) cubed Beet-Cooked Octopus (above)

¼ cup (12 g) chopped scallion

Butter, for the pan

Saffron Aioli (page 186), for serving

Beet-Pickled Onion (page 187), for serving

Edible flowers, for garnish (optional)

TO MAKE THE OCTOPUS: Rinse the octopus under cold running water and remove the entrails, eyes, and beak. Place it in a large pot and add enough water to cover. Finely grate the beet directly into the pot and stir to distribute evenly. Bring to a boil over medium heat. Lower the heat to a simmer and cook until the octopus is tender and the thickest part of a tentacle can easily be cut with a knife, 40 to 60 minutes.

Remove the octopus from the hot water and rinse to remove the grated beet. Transfer the octopus to a bowl, drizzle with oil, and season with salt and pepper. Let sit at room temperature for 1 hour.

Starting with the larger parts, chop the octopus into ¼- to ½-inch (6- to 12-mm) pieces until you have 1 cup (100 g). Set aside for the æbleskiver batter.

In a large frying pan over high heat, sear the remaining octopus until warm and crispy, 3 to 4 minutes on each side. Remove from the heat and set aside.

TO MAKE THE ÆBLESKIVER: In a medium bowl, combine the flour, charcoal powder, and salt and mix well. Set aside.

In another bowl, lightly mix together the stock and eggs with a fork. Pour the mixture over the dry ingredients and whisk quickly until just combined. Gently fold in the reserved cubed octopus and the scallion and try not to stir the batter again after this.

Heat the æbleskiver pan over low to medium heat with ½ to 1 teaspoon of butter in each cavity. Using an ice cream scoop or a spoon, fill each cavity almost to the top.

Cook until a crust forms on the batter. Using a thin wooden skewer, turn the æbleskiver 90°, letting the batter spill over. Once a skin has formed, the æbleskiver will turn easily. Turn again in a different direction and then a last time to close up the sphere. Spin the æbleskiver around until evenly golden brown and a toothpick inserted into it comes out mostly clean. Serve right away or keep the æbleskiver warm in a 200°F (100°C) oven.

TO SERVE: Serve the æbleskiver with the seared octopus, saffron aioli, and beet-pickled onion. Garnish with edible flowers (if using).

CLASSIC AIOLI

Makes about 1 cup (240 ml) | GF | NF | VG

1 large egg yolk, at room temperature

2 teaspoons fresh lemon juice

1 or 2 garlic cloves, minced

1 cup (240 ml) grapeseed oil

¼ teaspoon salt

Pinch of cayenne pepper

Combine the egg yolk, lemon juice, and garlic in a food processor and pulse until smooth and creamy. A hand blender can also be used. With the processor running, slowly drizzle in the oil and continue to process until thick and creamy. Taste and season with salt and cayenne pepper as needed. Transfer to a jar with a lid and refrigerate until ready to use or for up to 1 week.

VARIATIONS

VEGAN AIOLI: Omit the eggs and replace it with ½ cup (120 ml) of soy milk.

SAFFRON AIOLI: Crumble a pinch of saffron threads into 2 teaspoons of hot water and let soak for 10 minutes. Add the saffron water to the classic aioli and mix well.

ROASTED GARLIC AIOLI: Squeeze out 1 head of Roasted Garlic (page 159) and mash the cloves with a fork. Add the garlic to the classic aioli and mix well.

PESTO AIOLI: Stir ¼ cup (65 g) of Pesto (page 156) into the classic aioli and mix well.

BEET-PICKLED ONION

Makes about 2 cups (210 g) | GF | NF | V

1 red onion

1 red beet

¼ cup (60 ml) red wine vinegar

½ cup (120 ml) water

2 tablespoons sugar

Slice the onion very thin and place in a bowl or jar.

Coarsely grate the beet into a small saucepan and add the vinegar, water, and sugar. Bring to a boil over medium heat. Remove the pan from the heat and stir until the sugar has dissolved. Set aside to cool until lukewarm.

Strain the beet liquid through a cheesecloth and pour the liquid over the sliced onion. Refrigerate for up to 2 weeks.

INDEX

ACKNOWLEDGMENTS

A huge thank you, and tusen tack, to my extraordinary friends, family, coworkers, mentors and publishing team. Your unwavering support and endless sources of inspiration keep amazing me. This book would not be here without you. Thank you for your patience, for contributing recipes, testing recipes, tasting recipes, brainstorming sessions, and for following me outside the lines. Thank you to The Collective Book Studio for believing in this concept, and for supporting and guiding me into the professional world of book publishing.

Special thank you to Pappa, Mamma, Bengt Gerre, Malin Henriksson Pratt, Petra Henell, Wayne Maness, Mimmi Nordholm, Johanna Olin, Ylva Karlsson, Alva Gerre, Isak Gerre, Katarina Blom, Anna-Karin Persson Haraldsson, Annicka Haraldsson, Malin Van Dellen, Peter Van Dellen, Ulrika Gyllstad, Susanne Demåne, Lovisa Alsén, Patti Low, Mollie Low, Tanya Odisho, Jonas Gerre, Cia Gerre, Inga-Lill Karlsson, Ethan, Johan, Kaj & Axel Nordholm, Annelie Rosenquist, Niklas Mohlin, Amanda Benbow, Nancy Chin, Holly Muckelroy, Sarah Bresler Baugh, Melissa Kirk, Alexia Chimenti, David & Jason Trevino, Amy Treadwell, Rachel Lopez Metzger and Angela Angel.

ABOUT THE AUTHOR

PIM PAULINE OVERGAARD—half Swedish and half Norwegian—was raised in Sweden, educated in Denmark, and now resides in San Francisco, California. With a passion for all things creative, Pim first gained recognition with her cartoon-style illustrated gift books, which have been translated into several languages. Currently, she focuses on cookbooks, reimagining classic recipes for various dietary needs, and blending her love for art and design in her culinary creations. Pim is also Head Designer at Williams Sonoma Home, where her handcrafted edible displays, like the Gingerbread Village, occasionally adorn their Union Square flagship store window.